Pennsylvania
Homeowner's Guide
To Solar Electricity

Pennsylvania Homeowner's Guide to Solar Electricity

Dr. Vera Cole

Cover by
George Retseck

Illustrations by
Dave Bascelli

The Mid-Atlantic Renewable Energy Association is a nonprofit organization, dedicated to informing and educating the public on renewable energy production, energy efficiency, and sustainable living through meetings, workshops, educational materials and energy fairs.

Published by
Mid-Atlantic Renewable Energy Association
Post Office Box 84
Kutztown, PA 19530

To purchase directly from the publisher, please order on-line at
www.themarea.org or contact **bookinfo@themarea.org.**

Author photo by Bonnie Charleston-Stevens

Printed in Pennsylvania, USA.

Printed on recycled paper containing 100% post consumer waste.

ISBN 978-0-615-31031-2

Contents

Acknowledgements .... *ix*

Foreword .... *xi*

Introduction .... **xiii**

Exclusive Companion Website xiv

SunnyMoney Estimator xiv

Mid-Atlantic Renewable Energy Association (MAREA) xv

Important Notice xv

Chapter 1. How does solar electricity work? **1**

Solar Modules and Arrays 1

Solar Electricity for Home Use 2

Grid-Tie Options 3

Power Outages and Battery Backup 3

Off-Grid 4

Chapter 2. Electricity Production and System Size **5**

🖥 Net Metering 5

Your Electricity Consumption 6

Units of Measure 6

Size Matters 7

🖥 Actual Generation 8

Solar Array Size: Power Rating (kW) 9

Solar Array Size: Physical Area (ft^2) 10

Chapter 3. Will solar electricity work on my property? **11**

🖥 Orientation and Magnetic Declination 12

The Orientation (Azimuth) of Your Array 14

The Angle (Tilt) of Your Array 15

Fixed-Tilt Arrays *15*

Adjustable-Tilt Arrays *16*

Contents

🖳 Shading 16

Array Placement Options 18

On the Roof *18*

In the Yard (on the Ground) *21*

Facing the Facts 23

Sizing the Spot 23

Some Special Considerations 24

🖳 Inverter 26

Location *26*

Data & Monitoring *27*

Replacement *27*

🖳 Production Meter 27

Chapter 4. Energy Conservation and the Environment 29

🖳 Energy Audits 29

🖳 Arranging an Energy Audit 30

🖳 Federal Tax Credits for Energy Efficiency 31

🖳 Solar Hot Water Savings and Incentives 31

🖳 Pennsylvania Act 129 32

Save Energy, Save Money 32

Chapter 5. Solar Electric System Costs and Incentives 33

🖳 SunnyMoney Estimator 34

System and Installation Costs 34

🖳 Pennsylvania Sunshine Solar Program 36

Estimating Full Project Cost 39

🖳 Federal Tax Credit 39

🖳 Final Word on Costs 41

The System That's Just Right for You 41

Important Considerations 42

Chapter 6. Savings on Your Electric Bill........................ **43**

Rate Caps 43

   How do rate caps work? 45

   Energy Choice.. 45

   After Rate Caps Do Expire............................. 47

Smart Metering and Time-of-Use Pricing 48

Future Electricity Pricing, All Things Considered 49

Estimating Future Electricity Bill Savings..................... 50

Chapter 7. Renewable Energy Credits (RECs)................ **52**

Selling RECs is Selling the Green 53

Voluntary and Compliance REC Markets 53

Counting Your RECs.. 56

How RECs are Bought and Sold.................................. 57

REC Aggregators 58

REC Prices 59

S-REC Market LIFE 60

Estimating Your Income from RECs.............................. 60

   Important Note about RECs and Taxes 61

Chapter 8. For Love *and* Money? **62**

Environment 62

Home Improvement 63

Patriotic.. 63

Self Reliance 64

Certainty 64

Contents

Financial Analysis... 65
   Payback Period 65
   Simple Return on Investment (ROI) 66
   The Time Value of Money 66
   Internal Rate of Return (IRR) 68
   Net Present Value (NPV) 68
   "Price to Beat," the known price of your solar electricity.... 70

Chapter 9. Installation Process.. **71**
Before Contacting an Installer 71
   Contact Installers and Obtain Proposals............................. 71
   Proposals 72
   Select Installer and Proposal 72
   Before Installation.. 74
   Pennsylvania Solar Rebate: Pre-Approval............................ 74
   Grid Interconnect Application... 75
   Local Permits and Zoning Approvals 75
During Installation 75
   After Installation 75
   Local Inspections and Zoning Approvals 75
   Grid Interconnect Completion... 75
   Pennsylvania Solar Rebate: Request Reimbursement 75
   Federal Income Tax Credit.. 77
   RECs... 78
Epilogue... 79

Celebrating Local and Green.. **80**

Acknowledgements

Heartfelt gratitude to Bill Hennessy whose solar energy brilliance and passion for simply doing good inspired and motivated me every step of the way. As technical advisor, his guidance throughout this project was invaluable.

Special thanks to Tim Mahoney for topnotch editing and a manuscript that's clear and friendly.

Much appreciation to George Retseck for a beautiful cover by which I hope you'll judge this book!

Many, many thanks to Dave Bascelli for illustrations worth a thousand words and the web work that'll keep us all connected.

And sincere thanks to the many other friends of the earth and friends of MAREA who helped make this book better, including Patt Bossert, Bonnie Charleston-Stevens, Colleen Clemens, Trey Cole, Phil Jones, Janet Seggern and Marty Simon.

Green gratitude to Liz Choi of Five Thousand Forms for partnering with MAREA to make this an environmentally responsible project, beginning to end.

And of course, great appreciation to the Mid-Atlantic Renewable Energy Association's many members and incredibly talented and committed leadership for taking the plunge with me and publishing this book.

Foreword

When Vera Cole became interested in renewable energy, Jimmy Carter was president. Then a young engineering student, the challenge to her generation was to become independent from the whims of OPEC. Developing our country's abundant supply of coal was often touted as the key to independence. Commercial scale photovoltaics were a dream and the emphasis was on solar hot water.

It's topsy-turvy to today—coal has a leading role in the degradation of our environment and progress in developing inverters has led to a thriving photovoltaic industry. Predications are for the Mid-Atlantic region to exceed California's solar installations in the next five years.

Though seldom discussed in the 1970s, climate change now looms a larger issue than when OPEC was a few guys setting the price of crude while drinking coffee in Vienna. Little progress has been made to become energy independent or curb greenhouse gas emissions. Our dependence on foreign sources of fossil fuel is bigger than ever and we're just leaving behind years of denial regarding climate change.

Enter solar and its promise for the future—renewable, non-polluting and abundant.

"And what is the use of a book, without pictures or conversations?" asked Alice at the beginning of her wonderland journey.

This book is filled with facts, yet beyond the numbers and rules for going solar in Pennsylvania, we remember that civilization was solar-powered for the last 10,000 years and only in the last 300 have fossil fuels made an impact on our culture.

This is a practical book that will show you how to get from wherever you are to solar, but we're also offering it as an aid to reconnecting with our solar legacy and resuming our role as stewards of the environment.

To answer Alice, we hope the book will lead to conversations that go in the direction of a renewable, peaceful, sustaining world that respects all peoples.

Sometimes the questions are complicated, to paraphrase Dr. Seuss, but the answers are simple: Go solar, consume less, have fun.

"Unless someone like you cares a whole awful lot, nothing is going to get better. It's not."
The Lorax.

Bill Hennessy
Executive Director
Mid-Atlantic Renewable Energy Association

Introduction

Welcome to the exciting world of solar electric in Pennsylvania. Seriously, it is exciting! Consider all that's happening right here, right now: state rebates, federal tax credits, renewable energy credits (RECs), electricity price caps expiring and a planet in peril. Oy. In fact, maybe a little too exciting...or too confusing.

This book will explain, in plain language, what a Pennsylvania homeowner needs to know before purchasing and installing a solar electric system. It will help you answer these questions:

∞ How do solar electric systems work?

∞ How much of my electricity bill could I eliminate?

∞ Will solar electric work on my property?

∞ What will it cost after new government incentives?

∞ What are RECs and can I sell mine?

∞ How much money will I save? Can I make?

∞ How much will it help the environment?

∞ How does the installation process work?

To answer these questions, we'll dig into the details of how solar electric systems work, how big they are and where to put them, net metering, the Pennsylvania rebate program, the federal tax credit, energy credits, price cap expirations, the environmental impact, benefits/costs analysis, and the installation process itself.

This book is not meant as a do-it-yourself solar electric guide but instead tries to keep the level of detail to just what you need to know to make a good decision. The information in this book is specific to *residential solar electric* installations in *Pennsylvania*.

EXCLUSIVE COMPANION WEBSITE

With your purchase of this book, you gain access to an exclusive companion website with essential up-to-date information for residential solar electric installations in Pennsylvania. You can keep up with new and changing information on rebates, tax credits and state and federal programs. Tightly coupled to this book, the website contains chapter-by-chapter information and links to data that is likely to change and on-line resources, including certified installers, rebate levels, calculators, program requirements, downloadable forms and documents, reference material and more.

Throughout the book, a ![] marks sections where important information is available on the website.

To obtain the password and access the website, you'll need to have a copy of the book nearby. Then go to **www.themarea.org** and follow the links there.

SUNNYMONEY ESTIMATOR

Also on-line to accompany the text of this book is the SunnyMoney Estimator. This tool has been developed specifically for residential solar electric installations in Pennsylvania. It uses up-to-date information for Pennsylvania and national solar electric incentives applicable to residential installations. Use SunnyMoney to estimate system size, system cost and environmental impacts, as well as annual and life-of-system estimates for savings and income, and financial analysis.

SunnyMoney is also available at **www.themarea.org**.

MID-ATLANTIC RENEWABLE ENERGY ASSOCIATION (MAREA)

This book is published by the Mid-Atlantic Renewable Energy Association (MAREA), a nonprofit organization, dedicated to informing and educating the public on renewable energy production, energy efficiency, and sustainable living through meetings, workshops, educational materials and energy fairs. For more information, see **www.themarea.org.**

MAREA is widely known for its Pennsylvania Renewable Energy and Sustainable Living Festival, held each September in Kempton, PA. For festival news, see **www.paenergyfest.com.**

We hope this book will be a useful resource to homeowners considering solar electric and to installers, distributors and others in the industry who will benefit from an informed consumer.

IMPORTANT NOTICE

Every attempt has been made to provide information in this book and its companion website that is accurate and complete; however, neither the author nor publishers of this book make any claim to be providing professional advice on any topic including taxes, financial issues, legal issues, government regulations or programs, and solar electric system performance. Please seek professional counsel for advice in these areas.

We will however do our best to keep the facts straight, so please keep an eye on the website for updates. Thanks!

Chapter 1
How does solar electricity work?

How do solar electric systems work? They work great! (*baddaboom*)

Seriously, in the 1800s it was discovered that certain materials have the natural property of generating electricity when exposed to sunlight. But the amount of electricity was tiny. Over the years, vast improvements in materials and technology have led to the development of standard products that use this **photovoltaic (PV)** property to generate significant electricity directly from the sun, that's it. No moving parts required, no fuel and, in Pennsylvania, nearly no maintenance.

The photovoltaic material is typically silicon, an abundant natural resource, mixed with other natural materials to enhance its electricity-generating properties. The energy from the sun invigorates the photovoltaic material at the molecular level, causing electrons to break away, creating an electrical current. To conduct the current in a controlled and orderly manner, manufacturers package thin slices of photovoltaic material between layers of carefully designed conductors to form what is called a **solar cell**. But it still takes a lot of these cells to generate substantial amounts of electricity, so we usually buy groups of them packaged together.

SOLAR MODULES AND ARRAYS

The standard photovoltaic product provided by manufacturers is called a **solar or PV module (some say "panel").** A solar module is made up of individual solar cells wired and packaged together. Generally speaking, each module will have between 36 and 72 cells, measure about 2 to 3 feet by about 4 to 5 feet and weigh 30 to 40 pounds.

Multiple modules are usually installed in a group called a **solar array** (see Figure 1). This array is the wall of shiny panels you may see on a roof or yard. When sunlight hits an array, electricity is generated. The larger the array the more electricity you can generate.

SOLAR ELECTRICITY FOR HOME USE

The electricity generated by solar cells is in a form called "direct current" (DC). The electricity in your house, supplied by the utility company, is in a different form called "alternating current" (AC). This is the type of current used by your appliances and lights and anything else that you plug in. To make the energy from your solar array usable in your house, the current needs to be converted from DC to AC. This is done with an **inverter,** a small box usually mounted on a wall on the outside of the house or in a basement or utility room. Wiring will run from your PV array to the inverter. There, the DC is converted to AC.

The AC electricity coming out of the inverter is now ready for use in your house. Wiring will run from your inverter to your home's electrical panel (the metal box where all the circuit breakers are). The panel is where your house receives electricity from the power company, and now from your solar array too!

When your home electrical panel is getting power from the sun, your house uses the solar power *first* and then gets electricity from the power company only if more is needed. And in Pennsylvania, joy of joys, if your electrical panel is getting more power from the sun than your house needs, the excess power gets sent back to the power company, for full credit.

Figure 1. Solar cells, panels (modules) and array

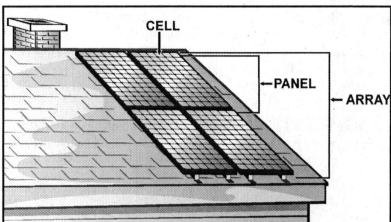

Figure 2. Grid-tied residential solar electric system

GRID-TIE OPTIONS
The system just described is called a **grid-tied** solar electric
system—your house is still connected to the utility company power
grid (see Figure 2). A house with no connection to a power
company is **off-grid**. In both cases, adding **battery backup** is an
option.

POWER OUTAGES AND BATTERY BACKUP
In a grid-tie system, you can think of the power company as a great
battery. When you need more power than you are solar generating,
your home gets electricity from the power company (at night, for
example). When you are generating more power than you need,
your home sends electricity to the power company for credit.

However, when the power company has an outage, you can't get
electricity from them *and* you don't have access to electricity from
your solar array. For safety reasons, to protect power company
workers, your solar array automatically disconnects during a power
outage so that no electricity reaches the power company lines...or
your house. Your inverter will do this automatically, within
milliseconds of the outage.

For these reasons, some people add a battery backup to their solar electric installation. This adds considerably to the cost and maintenance of a system and the decision to do so should be weighed carefully. Unless your power company is particularly prone to frequent and extended outages, battery backup is probably not an economically justifiable decision. In addition, the cost of a battery backup is not covered by the Pennsylvania Sunshine Rebate Program.

OFF-GRID

"Off-grid" means that your home is not connected to the power company and is completely self-reliant for electricity. This is most common in extremely remote areas where public services are less available and less reliable. Off-grid setups typically involve tight management of power consumption, extensive storage and coordination with other energy generating/saving systems.

Many of the concepts that will be discussed in this book do not apply to off-grid systems, including net metering and Renewable Energy Credits (RECs). If you are considering an off-grid setup, please keep these differences in mind.

Chapter 2
Electricity Production and System Size

If your solar array is generating more electricity than you are using, the extra will go to the power company. To make sure you are billed and credited fairly, Pennsylvania uses a system called "net metering."

NET METERING

In 2006, the Pennsylvania Public Utility Commission adopted the first standards for **net metering.** This established rules for how the power company handles your bill when you are generating some or all of your own electricity. The rules were amended in 2007 and revised rules went into effect in November of 2008.

Net metering means that your power company must keep track of the flow of electricity in two directions—how much they send to your house *and* how much you send to them. As your house consumes electricity, it first uses the power coming from your solar array. When your solar array is not generating as much as you need, your house gets additional electricity from the power company. When your solar array is generating more than you need, your house sends electricity to the power company. ("The needle turns backwards.")

If during the course of a month you generate more than you use, the power company records this as Net Excess Generation (NEG) and carries it over to the next month. This is like having electricity in the bank. In months where you need more electricity than you generate, the power company lets you draw on the electricity you have in the bank from previous months. Once that's used, you buy electricity from the power company.

Once a year, the power company settles up with you. If you still have NEG (electricity in the bank), they pay you for it. (You get full retail value for generation and transmission, not distribution. These terms are explained in Chapter 6.) In Pennsylvania, this settlement happens each year at the end of May.

For off-grid systems, with no connection to a power company, net metering does not apply.

How could net metering work for you?

To answer this, you'll need to consider how much electricity you use and how much you could generate.

YOUR ELECTRICITY CONSUMPTION

Your electricity use probably varies widely month to month and season to season. Often, electricity use is higher in the summer when people are using air conditioning. But, if your house is heated with electricity, your winter bills may be higher. The beauty of net metering is that you can plan your system based on the electricity you use during a full year, not on monthly demand.

How much electricity does your home consume in a year?

The best way to find this info is on your power bill or from your power company. If you look closely at your bill, you should find your total annual electricity usage, measured in kWh (kilowatt-hours).

It may be called something like "Last 12 months Use" or "Total Annual kWh Usage" or "Yearly Use."

If you do not find it, or are unsure, call your power company or check your account information on-line, if available. *This information is essential for making an informed decision about solar electricity.*

My home's annual electricity usage:

_____ kWh

UNITS OF MEASURE

Kilowatt-hours (kWh) is a measure of the **energy** used. **Power**, on the other hand, is a rate of energy conversion. Power is measured in Watts (W). A kilowatt is 1,000 Watts. A megawatt is one million Watts.

Think of a light bulb rated at 100 Watts. This is the power rating for the bulb. It tells us how much electricity it can transform into light and heat over a given amount of time. If left on for one hour, this bulb will use 100 Watt-hours (Wh) of energy.

In the same amount of time, a 100 W bulb will use four times as much energy as a 25 W bulb. If you leave them both on for one hour, the first bulb uses 100 Watt-hours (Wh) of energy and the second one uses 25 Watt-hours of energy. After 3 hours, it's 300 Wh and 75 Wh.

Your power company charges you based not on how many light bulbs you have, but on how much energy they use while you have them on.

Similarly, your solar array will be rated in Watts, like a light bulb, indicating the array's rate of energy conversion. Called a **power rating**, this is the rate at which your solar array can turn energy from the sun into electricity. For example, a 5 kW array can convert twice the energy in the same amount of time as a 2.5 kW array.

Sunlight on a solar array is like turning on the switch of a lamp. While sun is hitting the solar array, it generates electricity at a rate based on its power rating. The longer it is "on" and the bigger its power rating, the more sunlight it will convert to electricity.

SIZE MATTERS

Generally speaking, the larger your solar array the greater its power rating—the more solar cells, the more electricity.

There is variation in the electricity-generating capacity of different modules depending on who made them and how, and the underlying technologies (for example, single-crystal, polycrystal/multicrystal, ribbon and thin film silicon).

Nonetheless, for planning and estimating purposes, there is an accepted relationship between a solar array's size and its power rating. A rule of thumb is that **one square foot of solar array yields about 10 W of power**.

But how much electricity will an array actually generate? This depends on the amount and strength of sunlight. And that depends on where you live.

🖳 ACTUAL GENERATION

The National Renewable Energy Laboratory provides an on-line calculator for determining the energy production of solar electric systems throughout the world, based on long-term weather data. The on-line tool is called **PVWatts** ™. In their words: "This calculator allows homeowners, installers, manufacturers, and researchers to easily develop estimates of the performance of hypothetical PV [solar electric] installations."

PVWatts tells us that in Harrisburg, for example, a typical 1-kW array facing south with no shading will generate 1,193 kWh per year. This is based on historical weather data for Harrisburg, as well as standard derating factors for loses related to module variations, wiring, connections and the inverter. In Philadelphia, this same array is expected to generate about 1,206 kWh per year. Table 1 shows estimates for the amount of electricity a typical 1-kW array will generate each year at major Pennsylvania cities.

Table 1. AC electricity generation by location
These numbers are for the performance of a typical 1- kW solar array facing south with no shading and the amount of sunshine historically available at these locations.

	AC Electricity Generation (kWh/yr)
Allentown	1,184
Bradford	1,142
Erie	1,116
Harrisburg	1,193
Philadelphia	1,206
Pittsburgh	1,099
Wilkes-Barre	1,113
Williamsport	1,105

Source: National Renewable Energy Laboratory, PVWatts, Version 1

SOLAR ARRAY SIZE: POWER RATING (KW)

Remember the light bulbs with power ratings of 25 W and 100 W? Your solar electric system will have the same kind of rating indicating its capacity to turn sunlight into electricity. The higher the rating, the more electricity your solar electric system can produce in a given amount of time.

☑ **Power Rating.**

To estimate the power rating needed to fully eliminate your power bill, divide the annual electricity needed (kWh) by the AC Electricity Generation factor from Table 1. The answer will be in kW.

For example, the typical non-electrical-heating residence in Pennsylvania uses around 9,000 kWh per year. Let's pick somewhere central and say this home is in Harrisburg. To fully cover your annual electricity requirements in the Harrisburg area with solar electric, you would need an array with a power rating of about:

$$\frac{9000 \text{ kWh/yr}}{1{,}193 \text{ kWh/yr/installed kW}} = 7.54 \text{ kW}$$

Power rating needed to eliminate my entire electric bill:

_____ kW

SOLAR ARRAY SIZE: PHYSICAL AREA (FT^2)

We can expect one square foot of a typical residential solar module to have a power rating of about 10 W. This can be expressed as 1 ft^2/10 W or 1 ft^2/0.01 kW.

☑ **Array Size.**
To determine the approximate size of a solar array, divide the power rating by 0.01. The answer will be in ft^2.

Continuing the example above,

$$7.54 \text{ kW} \quad \text{x} \quad \frac{1 \text{ ft}^2}{0.01 \text{ kW}} \quad = \quad 754 \text{ ft}^2$$

If it helps you picture the size of this area, you can convert this number to an equivalent number of parking spaces by dividing by 160.

$$754 \text{ ft}^2 \quad \text{x} \quad \frac{1 \text{ parking space}}{160 \text{ ft}^2} \quad \sim \quad 5 \text{ parking spaces}$$

Array size needed to eliminate my entire electric bill:

_____ ft^2

Chapter 3
Will solar electricity work on my property?

By now you should have a good estimate of the physical size of a solar array that would be capable of generating sufficient electricity to meet your home's year-round consumption. Let's now look at issues and options for installing this array.

The most important considerations for where to place a solar array on your property are:

∞ **Azimuth (orientation)**—the direction it faces, such as south or southeast.

∞ **Tilt (angle)**—the angle of the array relative to the ground, measured in degrees (for example, 45°)

∞ **Shading**—available sunlight that is blocked from reaching the array

Solar cells convert energy from the sun into electricity. The more energy they get from the sun, the more electricity they generate. They get the most energy when the sun rays are hitting them perpendicular, head on, right in the eye.

As the earth spins and revolves through the days and the year, our angle to the sun is constantly changing. Each morning it appears in

Figure 3. Azimuth (orientation) and tilt (angle)

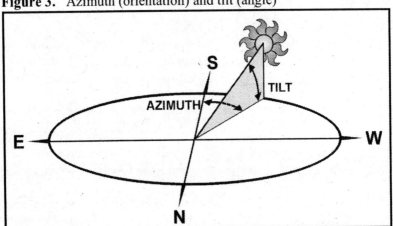

the east, sinking later in the west. In the summer, it travels this daily path high in the sky, in the winter it travels much lower.

When we position a solar array, we are trying to expose the cells to as much head-on sunlight as possible, keeping in mind these ever-changing angles. We plan the orientation and tilt of the array and monitor for obstructions that block (shade) sunlight from reaching the array.

Stand in your yard (when the neighbors aren't watching) and spread your arms at shoulder height, straight and wide. Turn so your left hand is in the direction the sun rises and your right hand in the direction the sun sets. You are now facing south. This is your orientation or azimuth. Lean slightly back or forward and you are adjusting your angle or tilt. These are the directional factors to consider when it comes to finding a spot for your solar array.

Your solar array operates most efficiently when sunlight strikes the surface as directly as possible. We seek to maximize this through orientation and tilt, and by avoiding shade.

🖳 ORIENTATION AND MAGNETIC DECLINATION

The ideal orientation of a solar array is **true south**. To find true south with certainty and to gain a better understanding of the orientation of your property and the structures on it, you may want to consider getting a compass. It's simple to use and interesting, and the grandkids love it! A compass is easily acquired and suitable ones cost less than $15. Be sure to get one with adjustable declination, as described below.

The needle on a compass points to magnetic north (the opposite direction of **magnetic south**). Magnetic north is slightly different than true north due to a natural phenomenon known as **magnetic declination**, which varies location to location.

To identify true south, a compass (or its reading) needs to be adjusted for local magnetic declination. The National Geophysical Data Center provides an on-line resource that computes the estimated value of magnetic declination for a location by zip code.

	Zip Code	Estimated Magnetic Declination
Allentown	18101	12°11' W
Bradford	16701	10°29' W
Erie	16501	9°30' W
Harrisburg	17101	11°12' W
Philadelphia	19107	12°11' W
Pittsburgh	15219	9°6' W
Wilkes-Barre	18702	12°7' W
Williamsport	17701	11°24' W
Source: National Geophysical Data Center		

Table 2. Magnetic declination for Pennsylvania locations

If you have your own compass, you'll need to adjust it for your local declination. In Pennsylvania, our declinations are west. To set your compass for local declination, turn the dial as shown below, according to the estimated magnetic declination for your location.

Figure 4. Compass and declination setting

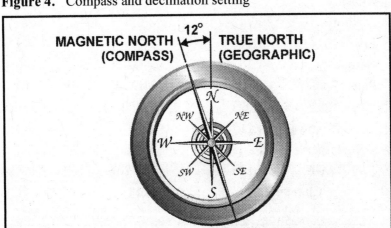

13

THE ORIENTATION (AZIMUTH) OF YOUR ARRAY

Most residential solar arrays will be installed so that they face one direction year round. Their orientation does not change. If a solar array is going to have one orientation year round, the one best direction is true south. But that is not always possible. How much does this matter?

Let's go back to PVWatts, the calculator on the National Renewable Energy Laboratory website that tells us how much electricity our system will generate for a given location. Table 3 shows the PVWatts results for a typical 1-kW array at locations across Pennsylvania, but this time facing three different directions: south, southeast (turned 45° east; 135°) and southwest (turned 45° west of true south; 225°)

On average, a solar array in Pennsylvania that faces a full 45° to the east or west of true south will generate about 6.5% less electricity per year than an array facing true south. This gives us more flexibility than we might have thought.

Table 3. Effects of orientation (azimuth) on AC generation

AC Generation (kWh/year) for Typical 1- kW Solar Array		
180° South	135° Southeast	225° Southwest
Allentown 1,184	1,105	1,097
Bradford 1,142	1,071	1,070
Erie 1,116	1,049	1,049
Harrisburg 1,193	1,120	1,106
Philadelphia 1,206	1,125	1,121
Pittsburgh 1,099	1,041	1,023
Wilkes-Barre 1,113	1,039	1,044
Williamsport 1,105	1,025	1,035
AVERAGE **1,145**	**1,072**	**1,068**
Average Change	**-6.4%**	**-6.7%**

Source: National Renewable Energy Laboratory, PVWatts, Version 1

THE ANGLE (TILT) OF YOUR ARRAY

In the summer the sun appears higher in the sky and in the winter it is lower. For maximum electricity generation, we want our solar array to be facing the sun as directly as possible. In the winter we would want it steeper and in the summer we'd want it flatter.

Residential solar arrays may have a **fixed tilt** (they are at one angle all the time), especially if they are on the roof, or may have a manually **adjustable tilt angle**. We will discuss tracking systems that automatically move an array later in this chapter.

Fixed-Tilt Arrays

For a fixed array, the one best angle for electricity generation year-round is about the same as the latitude of your site. (This works out, based on the angle of the sun in the sky above us.) In Pennsylvania, latitudes are around 40°. How important is it that the array be tilted at exactly this angle? Once again, let's use PVWatts.

Table 4 gives the PVWatts results for a typical 1-kW array facing south at locations across Pennsylvania, but this time with the array tilted at four different angles: an angle equal to the site's latitude, flatter than latitude (-15°), steeper than latitude (+15°) and flat.

Table 4. Effects of tilt (angle) on AC generation

AC Generation (kWh/year) for Typical 1- kW Solar Array				
	Latitude	Latitude-15°	Latitude+15°	Flat
Allentown	1,184	1,180	1,127	1,016
Bradford	1,142	1,144	1,083	1,004
Erie	1,116	1,131	1,043	1,012
Harrisburg	1,193	1,190	1,134	1,032
Philadelphia	1,206	1,199	1,150	1,034
Pittsburgh	1,099	1,107	1,033	990
Wilkes-Barre	1,113	1,120	1,051	984
Williamsport	1,105	1,109	1,044	971
AVERAGE	**1,145**	**1,148**	**1,083**	**1,005**
Average Change		0.2%	-5.4%	-12.2%
Source: National Renewable Energy Laboratory, PVWatts, Version 1				

In Pennsylvania, based on the data in Table 4, setting the array at a somewhat lower angle year round has very little effect on the amount of electricity generated. Setting an array at a steeper fixed angle has a greater effect, but still only a loss of 5% at a tilt 15° greater than latitude.

Adjustable-Tilt Arrays

The purpose of an adjustable tilt is to change the angle of the array with the seasons. The sun is higher in the summer, so a flatter tilt produces more electricity. The sun is lower in the winter, so a steeper tilt is better. To change the tilt of a manually adjustable array, a home owner (or professional) unlocks the array, and lifts or lowers it for the season.

If a homeowner chooses to do this, the summer angle should be the latitude-15° and the winter angle should be latitude+15°. This will result in the panel receiving about 3% more solar energy per year.

 SHADING

It is the nature of solar modules (having to do with the way the solar cells are connected to one another) to be *extremely* sensitive to shade. All solar modules are affected differently, but estimates for the impact of shade can be as high as 75% loss of power for the *entire module* when just one cell is shaded. More than 90% of power could be lost when three cells are shaded.

Your solar array should be located where it will have no shade between the hours of 9 a.m .and 3 p.m., year round.

Research to reduce this shade sensitivity is advancing, but products with substantially improved shade handling are not available for the residential market.

The change of the sun's angle causes different shading during the course of the year, in addition to the changes that happen throughout each day. A tree next to your solar array may be no problem in the summer, but a significant one in the winter. A nearby structure or pole may not be a problem most of the time, but cause significant morning shade in certain months.

But don't worry, you don't need to spend a year standing in the yard watching the shadows move (but it's good work, if you can get it!).

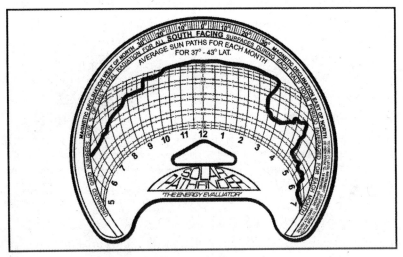

Figure 5. PathFinder shading analysis

There are clever systems available that project year-round shading for a specific location based on a one-time on-site reading. The more commonly used and accepted of these tools are the Solar PathFinder, Acme Solar Site Evaluation ASSET and SunEye.

Each of these tools has a measurement system to use the data from a one-time reading at your site to estimate the amount of shading hour by hour and month by month, year round. The tools document nearby obstructions—trees, structures, telephone poles, etc.—and gauge their shading impact throughout the year.

These tools are cleverly designed, not too hard to use, and provide new insight into the nature of your property. But it is not necessary, or even recommended, that you buy or learn to use one. Your installer, or other professional, will use one of these tools to document the year round "solar availability," "solar access" or "percent shading" for your site.

To emphasize how critical shading is, the Pennsylvania Sunshine rebate *requires* the submission of solar analysis documentation showing that a minimum of 80% available annual sunshine will reach the array. Solar electric generation will be greatly improved by percentages closer to 100%. Shading should be avoided to the fullest extent possible.

17

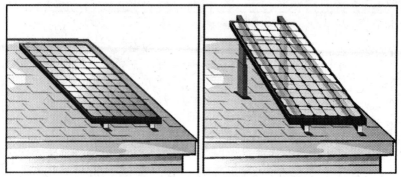

Figure 6. Flush and tilt-up roof mounts

ARRAY PLACEMENT OPTIONS

A solar array needs a large unshaded, south-facing area on your property. Generally your best bet is either a roof or the yard.

There are other possibilities, such as a carport roof or trellis, which may involve new construction. But let's consider the more common (and less expensive) options.

On the Roof

If, you have a significant roof area that faces south and is unshaded, it is probably your first choice for locating the solar array. It is out of the way and often the least expensive approach.

Typically, your installer will use an aluminum racking system to mount the system on your roof. The racking system is fastened to (through) your roof in multiple locations. The racking sits about 2 to 6 inches above the roof so air can circulate beneath the modules to help cool them. (Interestingly, the photovoltaic effect that produces electricity from sunlight works better at lower temperatures.)

Roofs and the Tilt of Your Array

Usually the array racking is installed parallel to the roof (the entire array is the same few inches above the roof), and this is called a **flush mount** rack. When the solar racking is installed at an angle to the roof (one end of the array is closer to the roof than the other), it is called a **tilt-up** rack. The tilt may be adjustable.

In the more common case of flush-mounted roof arrays, the slope of your roof determines the tilt angle of your array.

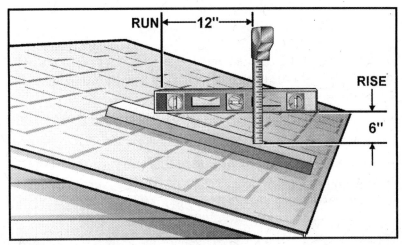

Figure 7. Roof rise & run

But what is the angle of your roof?

The angle of a roof is called its **pitch** and is typically measured as the number of inches it rises for every 12 inches of length. This measure is often referred to as "rise over run." (A 6/12 pitch means the roof gets 6 inches higher with each horizontal foot.)

For those of you who remember your high school trig, the rise-over-run measure for slope can be converted to degrees. Some common roof pitches are converted in Table 5.

Table 5. Roof pitch and corresponding tilt angle

Roof Pitch (Rise/Run)	Tilt Angle
4/12	18.4°
5/12	22.6°
6/12	26.6°
7/12	30.3°
8/12	33.7°
9/12	36.9°
10/12	39.8°
11/12	42.5°

Conventional roof slopes range between 4/12 (18°) to 9/12 (40°) range. Across Pennsylvania, latitude, which is the ideal year-round tilt for an array, varies near 40°, so the slope of a typical roof is flatter than ideal. But, we determined earlier that setting an array at an angle slightly flatter has little negative effect on total annual generation.

Bottom line: installing a solar array at the same slope as your roof is generally a-okay.

Considerations for Roof-Mounted Systems

Roof Material. Composite or "asphalt" shingles are easiest for solar mounts. Tile or slate roofs can require special consideration. Dark metal roofs can pose heat-related challenges.

Roof Condition. The modules in your solar array are guaranteed for 25 years, and will likely work far longer than that. (There is some loss of performance over time, about 1% a year, due to age-related deterioration on the surface of the module.) The roof where the array will be located should be in very good condition. Replacing the roof will require removing and reinstalling the array.

Tilt-Up Racking. For most small scale residential PV installations in Pennsylvania, tilt-up racking on a south facing roof will not significantly improve performance. In some cases, tilt-up racking may be used on a roof to change both the tilt angle and orientation of the array. These designs need to be considered on a case-by-case basis. Structural issues could be introduced if the array size and angle create a sail effect. If space allows, adding additional modules will compensate for less-than-perfect orientation or angle.

Weight. Typically, a fully installed roof-mounted solar array weighs 3 to 5 pounds per square foot. This is about the same as 2 to 4 inches of snow, or ½-inch to 1 inch of ice. The Uniform Construction Code requires that residential roofs be designed to support at least 75 pounds per square foot. The weight of a solar array presents little challenge to a sound roof.

Cleaning. In Pennsylvania, we get enough rain and snow to keep the arrays clean, without washing them ourselves. Getting up on the roof to perform maintenance is generally not needed. It is important that the solar array be free of dust and debris, and this should be taken into consideration if there are any special circumstances near your location.

Snow and Ice. Solar arrays are installed on the sunnier side of the house, have dark smooth surfaces and are mounted on an angle. Generally speaking, in Pennsylvania environments, snow and ice will melt and slide off. It's possible, in some areas, that ice or snow could accumulate and interfere with system performance. In those cases, access to a roof-mounted system may be difficult. Usually the need to reach an array for purposes of snow removal is not a factor in deciding whether to locate the array on a roof.

Aesthetics. Are you going to be pleased with the way the solar array looks on your roof? This is a matter of personal taste. Solar modules usually have a dark surface so your array will look like a large glistening dark area on your roof. Look at pictures on-line. Drive by other installations in your area to picture how the installation will look on your property. The array will be less obvious on a higher roof, of course.

In the Yard (on the Ground)

Another option for locating your solar array is in an open area in your yard or elsewhere on your property. You'll need a large area with no shade. The array will need to face south and be tilted. There are two basic approaches to installing a solar array in the yard.

In a **ground-mount** setup, a support frame is built and installed on the ground, and a rack is attached to the frame. In a **pole-mount** setup, one large pole is installed and a specially designed rack is attached to the top. Modules are attached to the rack and the rack's tilt angle may be fixed or adjustable.

In both cases, modules are attached to the racking to create a solar array and the angle of the rack may be fixed or adjustable. The installation can be at any height, as long as the array is unshaded year around.

Considerations for Ground-Mounted Systems

Pole-mount vs. ground-mount. A single-pole mount requires a large pole and deep footing. Exactly how large and deep depends on the size of your system and the nature of the soil. Rocky terrains can

.Figure 8. Pole and ground mounts for the yard

present additional challenges for digging a deep footing. On the other hand, the frame support for a ground-mount rack has many smaller support posts sharing the load and set less deeply into the ground, but there are more of them, requiring a larger foundation.

Mowing. You'll probably want to keep the array area neat looking, so consideration should be given to mounting the array at a height that is easy to maintain around and under. Positioning the array slightly higher makes it less vulnerable to flying debris from mowers.

Distance. Wiring will need to run the distance from your array to the electrical panel (breaker box) for your property. Long distances add to the cost of the installation in terms of labor and materials associated with trenching, conduit and heavier wire.

Adjustable Tilt (Angle). A ground-mounted array is generally easily accessible, making manual seasonal adjustments of the tilt angle a reasonable option. Changing the tilt angle to make the array flatter in the summer and steeper in the winter will improve the amount of radiation available to the array for conversion to electricity by about 3%. A word of warning: if you miss a seasonal adjustment and leave the array at a low summer angle during the fall and winter, for example, the net effect could be negative. The tilt option is a design consideration to discuss with your installer, to decide if any additional cost is worth it to you.

Racking Material. The rack should be designed and constructed of materials to exceed the lifetime of the solar array, 25 years or more. Wood, even pressure treated, is not a good idea. Aluminum is the best choice.

FACING THE FACTS

After looking at your roof and yard, and considering orientation and shade, you have a rough idea of what areas may be best suited for solar, *if any*. Solar electric is absolutely unforgiving when it comes to shade. You *must* have a large area that is unshaded 9 a.m. to 3 p.m., year round. There's no getting around it.

If you don't, so sorry. Pass this book on to a friend. You may want to consider solar hot water, which is somewhat more forgiving. In any event, always, always continue to take energy conservation measures. It's the best and cheapest way to cut your power bill.

SIZING THE SPOT

If you do have a south-facing, unshaded sunny area, congrats! You'll want to get a rough idea of the size of the area, in square feet. Use a long measuring tape, or just walk it off. Most people have feet that are about a foot long—walk an imaginary tight rope, heel to toe, heel to toe. If it's on the roof, you don't have to get up there; just measure with a tape or your feet, the approximate length in both directions. Multiply the length of one side by the other, and you have an idea of the area size in square feet. Remember to measure only the part you believe to be fully unshaded, year round.

☑ **Site Area.**
   To estimate the size of an area where you think a solar array will work, multiply the length of the area by the width of the area, measured in feet. The answer will be in ft^2 (square feet).

For example,

30 ft x 12 ft = 360 ft^2

Array size that will fit on my property:

_____ ft^2

Based on its size, you can estimate the array's power rating. (Remember, this is like the wattage for a light bulb, except in reverse. The power rating indicates how much electricity an array can generate from available sunlight.)

☑ **Power Rating from Array Size.**
   To estimate the power rating (in kW), multiply the size of an array (in ft^2) times 0.01.

For example,

360 ft^2 x 0.01 kW/ ft^2 = 3.6 kW

Power rating of array that will fit on my property:

_____ kW

SOME SPECIAL CONSIDERATIONS
Tracking Systems
The systems described above have a fixed orientation—they always face the same direction—and have a fixed or manually adjustable tilt. These systems have no moving parts so there's far less that can go wrong or that needs to be tended. However, because the arrays

Figure 9. Tracking systems

are sitting still while the sun is moving in the sky they are usually not in the very best position to get the most energy from the available sun. Tracking systems are mounting systems that move the array to follow the sun. They are not generally warranted or cost effective for residential installations in our part of the country. Here's a quick look at what's available:

Active tracking systems are motor-driven mechanical systems that move a solar array to better follow the sun. **Single-axis active tracking systems** move the array east to west. **Dual-axis active tracking systems** move the array east to west daily and adjust the tilt for time of year. Naturally, these systems cost more and require on-going servicing and maintenance. Active tracking systems are better suited for optimizing large scale system performance, not for small residential installations.

Passive tracking systems are also mechanical systems that cause the array to move but instead of a motor they are driven by canisters of compressed gas that shift with temperature to redistribute weight, causing the system to move. Passive trackers can be slow to react in cold temperatures and arrays can be moved by high winds. They are not typically cost justified for small residential installations in Pennsylvania.

Alternative Photovoltaic (Solar Electric) Technologies
Different processing methods are used to produce three different types of photovoltaic products. A quick overview:

Monocrystalline solar modules are made from a single large silicon crystal. These modules are the most expensive but also more efficient. They convert more of the available energy from the sun to electricity and work better at high temperatures.

Polycrystalline solar modules are made from silicon that is formed into an ingot and sliced into cells. These cells typically are less efficient than monocrystalline.

With **thin film** (amorphous) technology, photovoltaic properties come in a film that is deposited on a substrate, such as glass, plastic or metal. It is both less expensive and less efficient than mono- or poly-crystalline products.

For residential applications we're looking to get the most energy production for the buck. Most often the best choice is polycrystalline. Thin-film, though tempting because of its low material cost per watt, requires a larger area and increased installation labor.

Building-Integrated Photovoltaics (BIPV)
Building materials, such as roofs, awnings, or skylights, that have built-in solar electric properties are called **building-integrated photovoltaics (BIPV)**. They use a thin-film technology described above. These specialized materials represent exciting new opportunities for residential solar electric but are not yet widely used.

⊞ INVERTER
In addition to an array of solar modules, the other main component of your system is an inverter. It is a wall-mounted box that typically has a small display screen.

Location
In our part of the country, inverters are typically installed in a utility room or cellar. If the unit is weatherproof, a protected area outdoors can work. Inverters are not usually installed in primary living areas

(because of size, appearance and maybe a little noise), but do need to be accessible.

Your inverter will have a Ground Fault Detector and Interrupter (GFDI) fuse to protect your system from ground faults. If it should blow, it can be easily replaced. (However, finding the ground fault itself requires a professional and can be time consuming.)

Some inverters have an internal cooling fan that makes a humming sound that some people find annoying. The air intake filter for the fan should be cleaned periodically to avoid overheating.

Your installer will recommend where to mount the inverter for the most efficient installation and best access. See the owner's manual provided with your system for details of operation.

Data & Monitoring
The inverter display will indicate performance status and provide a readout of operating parameters, including daily and accumulated energy production (kWh). You may find it convenient to have a remote display located in the kitchen or other living area where you can easily observe your system's performance. For this option, ask your installer about availability and cost.

Another option is to have your system's real-time performance data available on-line. Several inverter manufacturers have components and websites that let you view your system's data through a portal on the company's web site.

Replacement
The Pennsylvania rebate program requires a five-year manufacturer's warranty on inverters. An inverter normally lasts 10 to 15 years. It is likely that your inverter will need to be replaced during the life of your system.

PRODUCTION METER
A production meter is a separate meter, in addition to the one provided by your utility company, that is used to measure the electricity generated by your solar electric system. It is installed at your expense.

The Pennsylvania solar rebate program requires that a production meter be installed and that your installer report readings from this meter to the Department of Environmental Protection once a year for at least three years.

The production meter will need to be installed at a location between the inverter and your home's electrical panel.

Also, you will need bi-directional metering to keep track of the electricity you buy from the grid and send to the grid. This meter is provided by your utility company at no charge to you. In most cases it replaces your existing meter, but in some cases the utility may install a second meter.

Chapter 4
Energy Conservation and the Environment

Most of us find that to eliminate our entire electric bill we'd need a pretty big solar array. Huge, actually. So let's step back for a second.

The purpose of a residential solar electric system is to reduce the amount of electricity we buy from the grid.

But energy conservation does exactly the same thing, and often costs far less.

In 2008, 55% of the electricity generated in our region was fueled by coal, 35% was from nuclear plants and 7% from gas-powered sources. The remaining 3% was from hydroelectric, solid waste, wind and other. Solar doesn't register yet. According to the Environmental Protection Agency, every 1,000 kWh of electricity we don't buy from the grid results in 0.79 tons of avoided carbon dioxide emissions. It doesn't matter *how* we avoid buying it from the grid—simply using less electricity works just as well, if not better, for the environment than generating our own.

But cutting the amount of electricity we use is easier said than done. Where do you start? It is legitimately confusing—light bulbs (how much do they really matter?), replacing appliances, new windows, add insulation (where and how much?), phantom loads (what?), and so on. How do you spend your time and money in a way that will really make a difference?

⊞ ENERGY AUDITS

The best starting point is an **energy audit** of your home, either by a professional or yourself. The purpose of an energy audit is to identify energy-saving fixes that are no- or low-cost and to suggest other cost-effective improvements for saving energy.

Most residential energy consumption is for space heating (44%), followed by water heating (16%), air conditioning (8%), lighting (7%) and electronics (5%), according to a Department of Energy report for 2008. Notice this is *energy* consumption, which may involve sources other than electricity, such as oil for your furnace or gas for appliances.

Energy audits often start with the building envelope. You can think of this as everything that separates the inside of your house from the outdoors. Even small holes in the envelope cause drafts or leaking. The Department of Energy reports that the potential energy savings from reducing drafts may range from 5% to 30% a year. These drafts often found at electrical outlets and switch plates, window frames, baseboards, doors, utility chases to the attic and fireplace dampers. Professional auditors have systems and tools for identifying these leaks and recommending solutions that are often quick and easy.

Once the leaks are sealed, the next consideration is insulation. Your HVAC system should also be in good repair and well maintained. If it is more than 15 years old, it may pay to replace it with a newer, more efficient model.

Lighting loads may be reduced with more efficient bulbs, smaller bulbs, dimmer switches, timers, sensors and the age-old, "Turn the light off when you leave the room!"

Many appliances with built-in electronics, such as computers, DVD players, televisions, stereos and kitchen appliances use electricity even when they are turned off. These are called **phantom loads**. And, according to research funded by the Department of Energy, these loads make up approximately *five percent* of the residential electricity use in the US. To avoid this, you can simply unplug the appliance or plug it (and other appliances) into a power strip and then turn the power strip off.

An energy audit will provide direction on all these fronts and more.

ARRANGING AN ENERGY AUDIT

A qualified professional energy auditor will be certified by, one or both, the Building Performance Institute (BPI) and Residential Energy Services Network (RESNET). As with all contractors, check professional credentials and recent references.

In Pennsylvania we have the Keystone HELP Energy Efficiency Program for loans and rebates related to improving the efficiency of homes, including high efficiency heating, air conditioning, insulation, windows, doors, geothermal and "whole house" improvements. This program also sets forth energy audit requirements and auditor qualifications.

🖳 FEDERAL TAX CREDITS FOR ENERGY EFFICIENCY

The federal tax code provides for a Residential Energy Efficient Tax Credit, which pays 30% of the cost of qualified energy efficiency improvements up to a maximum of $1,500. Eligible technologies include water heaters, furnaces, boilers, heat pumps, air conditioners, building insulation, windows, doors, roofs, and circulating fans used in a qualifying furnace.

🖳 SOLAR HOT WATER SAVINGS AND INCENTIVES

Solar hot water (solar thermal) systems use warmth from the sun to heat water for use as either domestic hot water (for example, showers, sinks, washers) or for space heating. According to the Department of Energy, on average, if you install a solar water heater, your water heating bills should drop 50% to 80%.

The same Pennsylvania program that provides solar electric rebates also provides rebates up to $2,000 for solar thermal systems used for domestic hot water. The system installer must be on the Pennsylvania Department of Environment Protection's list of approved installers.

Similarly, the Federal Renewable Energy Tax Credit that applies to solar electric generators also has provisions for solar water heating. The tax credits are for 30% of the cost of eligible systems with no limit for systems placed in service after 2008. The equipment must be properly certified.

Both programs exclude solar thermal for heating swimming pools or hot tubs.

Solar hot water can provide greater energy savings in terms of bang for the buck than solar electric. It is recommended that a homeowner consider solar hot water heating prior to or in conjunction with an investment in solar electric.

PENNSYLVANIA ACT 129
In October 2008, Pennsylvania Act 129 was signed into law. Among other things it addresses the need for electric service that is "adequate, reliable, affordable, efficient and environmentally sustainable," greater adoption of energy efficiency and conservation measures and expanding the use of alternative energy.

Act 129 mandates that power companies with more than 100,000 customers must reduce consumption by 1% by May 2011 and 3% by May 2013. It also says they must reduce peak demand by 4.5% by 2013.

By the end of July 2009, power companies must file a plan for how they are going to achieve the required energy conservation. It is widely expected that these plans will include incentives and services to motivate homeowners to curb their electricity consumption. Stay tuned for promising opportunities on this front.

Act 129 also mandates plans for "smart meters" and time-of-use pricing, due August 2009 and January 2010, respectively. **Smart meters** are bi-directional meters that take readings at least once an hour so that utilities can track and bill for electricity based on how much you use *and when*. Setting prices higher during peak demand will encourage customers to shift usage to less expensive off-peak times and rates.

Because solar peak output generally coincides with peak system demand, time-of-use pricing is an especially promising development for solar generators.

SAVE ENERGY, SAVE MONEY
Though perhaps not as exciting as a big shiny array mounted on your roof or in your yard, energy conservation can provide outstanding savings in energy costs and for the environment. Any investment in solar electric generation should be coupled with energy-saving home improvements, including solar hot water, and individual behavior: for example, turning off lights and phantom loads, managing thermostats, and shifting usage to off-peak hours.

Chapter 5
Solar Electric System Costs and Incentives

The cost of your solar electric system is driven by the size of the system. When settling on the size of your system there are several factors to consider:

∞   What size (power rating) will it take to meet your home's full electricity needs?

∞   How much unshaded south-facing space do you have available for a solar array?

∞   What size suits your budget?

The right system for you will be the smallest answer to each of these three questions. It will be one that meets your needs, fits on your property and is within your budget.

In earlier chapters, you answered the first two questions. From Chapter 2, you know the approximate size and power rating of the array necessary to eliminate your entire electric bill. From Chapter 3, you know the estimated size and power rating of an array that will fit on your property. Which of these is smaller? For estimating costs, start with an array this size.

For estimating my costs & incentives:

Array size

_____ ft²

Power rating

_____ kW

The rest of this chapter will help you answer the third question, "What size of solar electric system meets my budget?"

▣ SUNNYMONEY ESTIMATOR

Good news: All the calculations from this point forward can be done for you automatically by the SunnyMoney Estimator, available on-line and free. You enter the size of the system you are considering and SunnyMoney performs all the calculations for you, making it quick and easy to compare costs and results for different size systems (but they still need to fit on your property!).

The methods and examples for calculating are shown in this book so you'll understand what's happening behind the scenes and be able to interpret the SunnyMoney results.

SYSTEM AND INSTALLATION COSTS

You will need an installer to give you an exact price for the installation of a new solar electric system. The price will depend on many factors including material costs, where and how your system will be installed and other considerations.

Your installer might give you a proposal with a breakdown that includes the costs of materials, labor, permits, and so forth. But generally speaking, the solar industry talks about installation prices in terms of "dollars per watt" or $/W. The Pennsylvania Sunshine Rebates are based on $/W.

The number of "watts" or "installed watts" used in cost calculations is the same as your array's power rating. Remember, 1 kW equals 1,000 W.

Generally speaking, the price of a solar electric system in Pennsylvania will probably be in the range of $7W to $10/W. For a 4 kW system this would be $28,000 to $40,000.

But don't stop breathing! This is before state and federal incentives which can be expected to reduce the total by over 50%. Plus, you will have electricity bill savings and the potential for REC income, all discussed in upcoming sections.

Usually, most of the cost of a system is in the components. Labor is likely a small portion of the overall cost. As the solar industry continues to mature, with new technology, higher volumes and greater competition, material and component prices are dropping.

Your cost will also be affected by where and how your pane be mounted and other site-specific factors.

Some things about your property that may increase costs:

∞ Long distances between your array and your home's electrical panel that may call for additional trenching and the use of more conduit and heavier wiring.

∞ Difficult area to access, such as a hard-to-reach roof.

∞ Upgrades to your electrical panel, if needed.

∞ Any special configuration, such as nonstandard geometrical modules and array placement.

Other items may also add to the costs:

∞ Battery backups, which require batteries, a charge controller, and a cabinet.

∞ Extra monitoring equipment and sensors.

∞ Tracking devices.

∞ Specialized building-integrated solar materials

In all cases, discuss with your installer the details of the pricing and be sure you understand the costs of choices you are making and any opportunities for reducing the price.

In Pennsylvania, homeowners now have access to two government incentives that significantly reduce the cost of solar electric: the Pennsylvania Sunshine Solar Program and the Federal Renewable Energy Tax Credit.

...IA SUNSHINE SOLAR PROGRAM

...nshine Solar Program" provides $100 million
..solar hot water for homeowners and small
..r electric portion began on May 18, 2009.

...tial details of the *residential, solar electric* portion
of this pr...

∞ It applies to PV systems with a DC power rating between 1 kW and 10 kW. Larger systems may participate, but will only receive rebates equivalent to the cost of the first 10 kW.

∞ Rebates start at $2.25 per watt and then drop in $0.50 increments as the program fills up. The price step-downs occur at 10-million-watt (10 megawatt) milestones. After rebates are issued for a total of 10 megawatts, the rebate level will drop to $1.75. After the next 10 megawatts, it will go to $1.25. After the next 10 megawatts, $0.75. No one knows how quickly these levels will be reached. Rebate applications will be handled on a first-come, first-served basis.

∞ The rebate cannot exceed 35% of the project cost.

∞ The person who installs your system must be on Pennsylvania's Department of Environmental Protection's list of installers approved for this rebate program.

∞ Your installer is required to perform a shade analysis of your proposed site and that analysis must show that 80% or more of the potential solar radiation at your location is not blocked from reaching your solar array.

∞ All components must be new and listed on the California Solar Initiative list.

∞ Application fee is $100.

∞ For applicants who qualify as low income, there is no application fee and a full 35% rebate. The qualifying income level for a family of four is currently $44,443.

∞ Applicants must be Pennsylvania residents and must live in the home where the system will be installed.

∞ If the solar electric system is part of, or simultaneous with, new construction, the initial construction process must be Energy Star qualified.

∞ The following are NOT covered: roof improvements, battery backups, vacation homes and investment properties

∞ The program is NOT retroactive. Systems must be installed, and all costs must be incurred, after the rebate program opened.

∞ If the project has a total cost of greater than $25,000, Pennsylvania's Prevailing Wage Act may apply. It is the responsibility of you, the recipient of the rebate, to know if this act applies to your project and to follow it if applicable. For more information, contact the Pennsylvania Department of Labor and Industry at (717) 705-7256 or (800) 932-0665.

∞ Applicants must not have any delinquent obligations to Pennsylvania, including state taxes.

∞ Installations must include a utility-grade production meter (new or refurbished) to measure your solar electric system's actual electricity generation. Your installer is required to report an annual reading from this meter to the Department of Environmental Protection for at least the first three years after the project is completed.

☑ **Pennsylvania Sunshine Rebate.**
To estimate your state rebate, multiply the system power rating (in kW, at most 10 kW) by 1,000 by the current rebate level (at this time, $2.25).

With a rebate level of $2.25 per installed Watt, for a 4 kW system, the rebate amount will be:

4 kW x 1,000 W/kW x $2.25/W = $9,000

Then double check to be sure the rebate doesn't exceed 35% of the full project costs. Your rebate will be the lesser of the two.

Nice! And we're still not done; read on.

Estimated Pennsylvania rebate for my system:

$ _____

ESTIMATING FULL PROJECT COST

To determine the Federal Tax Credit you will need the full project cost, or a good guess. This is the price you get from an installer, before the rebate and tax credit are taken into account.

☑ **Estimated Project Cost**

If you don't have a quote from an installer, you can estimate the installed unit cost to be in the range of $7 to $10/Watt. To estimate the full project cost, multiply the installed unit cost by the system's power rating (in kW) by 1,000.

For example,

$8.00/W x 4.2 kW x 1,000 W/kW = $33,600

My estimated project cost (before rebate and tax credit):

$ _____

🖳 FEDERAL TAX CREDIT

The Federal Residential Renewable Energy Tax Credit has been around since 2005, but recent changes starting in the 2009 tax year have greatly increased the savings to homeowners.

In the past, the credit was limited to $2,000. The 2009 American Recovery and Reinvestment Act changed this and now provides a tax credit for 30% of the cost, *with no cap*.

Furthermore, it appears that the basis for this credit is the full project cost, before the Pennsylvania Sunshine Rebate is subtracted.

Please note that tax law is tricky business and this is all new policy. This book does not represent official tax advice or direction. Please consult a professional tax advisor for guidance relative to your project and personal finances.

Here are essential details related to 2009 Federal Renewable Energy Tax Credit for *residential* systems:

∞ Applies to solar water heat, photovoltaics, wind, fuel cells, geothermal heat pumps, and other solar electric technologies.

∞ Tax credit for 30% of full project installation cost.

∞ Starting with 2009 tax year, no limit.

∞ Does not have to be primary residence.

∞ Tax credits can be carried over to succeeding tax year.

∞ Tax credit expires Dec 31, 2016.

☑ **Federal Residential Renewable Energy Tax Credit**
To estimate your federal tax credit, multiply the full project cost by 0.30.

For a 4.2 kW system at $8/Watt, the project cost would be $33,600. The Federal Tax Credit at 30% with no cap, would be:

$33,600 x   0.30 = $10,080

Estimated federal tax credit for my system:

$ _____

🖳 FINAL WORD ON COSTS

Assuming you meet all the qualifying criteria for the Pennsylvania and Federal incentives, the final cost for the installation of your residential solar electric system will be the amount quoted by your installer, minus 30% for the federal tax credit and minus $2.25 per watt (for now) for the state rebate. For example, you receive an installer's quote of $28,500 for a 3.6 kW system.

Installation Cost
> *Installer quote for 3.6 kW system* $28,500

Federal Tax Credit
> *30% of project cost ($28,500 x 0.30)*   - $8,550

Pennsylvania Rebate
> *3.6 kW x 1,000 W/kW x $2.25/W*   <u>- $8,100</u>
>   **$11,850**

THE SYSTEM THAT'S JUST RIGHT FOR YOU

To find the system size that's just right for you, start with your estimated project cost (before rebate and tax credit).

Calculate the Federal Tax Credit and subtract it. Then, calculate the state rebate and subtract it. How's that number?

If it's too much for your budget, make the system smaller, and try again. How's that?

This is easy to do with the SunnyMoney Estimator. Try different system sizes and see the results. Do this until you find the system that gives you as much energy as possible, still fits on your property and falls within your budget.

IMPORTANT CONSIDERATIONS

Okay! In the interest of responsible financial planning, here are a few more important considerations:

∞ **Pennsylvania will issue a Form 1099 for the amount of your solar rebate.** This book does not claim to be a tax guide or offer official tax advice, but it does appear that rebate money you receive from the Pennsylvania Sunshine Solar Program should be reported as income and will be subject to federal income taxes. At this point, Pennsylvania has not published a determination relative to rebates being subject to state income tax. Consider this possibility and consult a tax professional.

∞ Consider the timing of the cash flow. Unless you've worked out other arrangements, your installer is likely to expect final payment when the project is complete. You will need to wait for the rebate check from the state of Pennsylvania. Processing times for state reimbursements typically take 4 to 8 weeks. Your rebate processing will begin when the on-line request is complete and all additional materials have been received.

∞ The federal tax credit is just that, a *tax credit*, which means the federal government takes this money off your tax bill. In the example above, the tax you owe the federal government would be reduced by $8,550. Depending on your personal finances, it may take more than one year to use all of this credit. Contact a tax professional for details related to your filings.

∞ In Pennsylvania, solar electric systems generally need very little maintenance and the systems can be expected to operate for 25 years or longer. However, inverters generally last for 10 or 15 years. Currently, the rule of thumb for the cost of inverter replacement is about $700/kW. So, for our 3.6 kW system, we could be talking about another $2,500 in 10 or 15 years. However, technology is improving and component prices are currently dropping, making it difficult to estimate what the actual cost will be that far down the road.

Chapter 6
Savings on Your Electric Bill

In this chapter, we will consider how much this system will save you in future electricity bills.

The question is not complicated: how much electricity will I *not* have to buy from the power company and how much would it have cost? We can estimate fairly accurately the amount of electricity your system will generate over the next 25 years. The tricky part is estimating the future cost of electricity if you had to buy it from the power company.

Let's review a few basics:

∞   Solar electric systems have a lifespan of 25 years or more.

∞   Thanks to Pennsylvania's net metering standards, you do not have to time when your electricity is generated with when it is used. Credit for extra generation in one month is available to you the next month.

∞   In the rare case that your system has generated more electricity over the course of the year than you have used, the power company pays you at the "price-to-compare" rate. This includes generation and transmission components, but not the distribution component, of your electricity bill.

🔆 RATE CAPS

For most residents in Pennsylvania, "rate caps" on the price of electricity will expire at the end of 2009 or 2010. For about 15% of residents, this has already happened. To see where you fit in, check Table 6.

In general, "expiring rate caps" sounds like higher future electricity prices. And the higher the cost of electricity, the more money a solar electric system will save you.

But what will electricity prices really be in the future? If your rate caps have already expired, then you know what did or did not happen to your power bill, and it varied from region to region.

	Generation Rate Cap Status	% of PA Rate Payers
Allegheny Power (West Penn Power)	Dec 31, 2010	12.7
Citizens Electric Of Lewisburg	expired	0.1
Duquesne Light Company (DQE)	expired	10.6
Pennsylania Power Co. (PennPower) - FirstEnergy Co.	expired	2.8
Metropolitan Edison Company (Met-Ed) - FirstEnergy Co.	Dec 31, 2010	9.5
Pennsylvania Electric Company (Penelec) - FirstEnergy Co.	Dec 31, 2010	10.6
PPL Electric Utilities	Dec 31, 2009	24.6
PECO Energy Company - Exelon Company	Dec 31, 2010	27.8
Pike County Light & Power Co.	expired	0.1
UGI Utilities Inc.	expired	1.1

Table 6. Rate cap expiration schedule

For the 85% of us that are still under price caps, we don't know what's going to happen to prices when caps expire in our area. Speculation is rampant. Some say prices will rise a little, some say a lot, some say by a huge amount...and others say prices will fall.

🖥 How do rate caps work?

Take a look at your electricity bill and you'll see separate charges for Distribution, Transmission, Transition and Generation. This unbundling of services is a result of Pennsylvania's 1996 Energy Competition and Choice Act.

The Distribution and Transmission charges are for services provided by your local power company in delivering power to your home safely and reliably. These services and prices are regulated and will remain so. The expiration of rate caps will have no affect on the Distribution and Transmission charges on your power bill.

The Transition charges on your bill (also referred to as "stranded costs") are related to a settlement made with the power companies as part of the Energy Competition and Choice Act. When rate caps expire, the Transition charges will disappear from your power bill.

The Generation charges on your bill are for the production of the electricity you use. It is the rate cap on *these charges only* that is about to expire. When rate caps expire, the price you pay for electricity generation will no longer be fixed but will be set by your electric generation supplier.

These categories are summarized in Table 7.

🖥 Energy Choice

Electric generation supplier? Who is that? Another thing that the Energy Competition and Choice Act accomplished was to give customers the right to choose who generates the electricity they use. Your power company, the folks in charge of delivering your electric service, is determined by where you live, but you can choose who generates the electricity you buy.

Of course you have to choose from a list of qualified sources that serve your region. If you don't make a choice, then your power company buys the electricity on your behalf and charges you for it. In this case the power company is filling its role as the Provider of Last Resort.

Because generation prices have been set by rate caps, there's not been a lot of incentive for new suppliers to enter the market and try to compete on price. But, when rate caps expire, the theory is that

	Types of Charges on Your Electricity Bill				
	Customer	Distribution	Generation	Transition	Trans-mission
Reason for Charge	Flat fee to cover billing, meter reading, etc. (Not all charge this.)	Local lines & equipment to deliver electricity from high voltage transmission lines to your home	Actual production of electricity	Result of settlement with PUC, lets power company recover "stranded costs"	High-voltage lines & equipment used to move electricity from generator to distribution lines.
Service Provider	Your local power company, determined by where you live	Your local power company, determined by where you live	You have the right to **choose** who generates your electricity. Limited to available suppliers in your area. If you do not make a choice, your power company buys power for you	Not really a service, but a charge from your local power company, determined by where you live	Your local power company, determined by where you live
Pricing-- Under Rate Caps	Regulated by PA Public Utility Commission (PUC).	Regulated by PA.	If your power company is procuring electricity for you, the price is capped. If you have made a choice, the price is set by your chosen supplier.	These costs expire over time. Schedule depends on individual power company.	Federal Energy Regulatory Commission (FERG) sets guidelines for these costs. They are regulated by PA PUC.
Pricing-- After Rate Caps	No change	No change	**Market price** as set by generation supplier--either the supplier you choose or your power company	**Fully eliminated** when rate caps expire.	No change

Table 7. Pennsylvania electricity bill pricing

more suppliers will enter the picture, competition will heat up and prices will fall.

At this point, however, the number of alternative suppliers remains limited, even in areas where rate caps have expired. It's hard to predict what the impact of electricity supplier competition on prices will be.

🖳 After Rate Caps Do Expire

What has happened to prices in areas where rate caps have expired? Results have been mixed.

Data from the Pennsylvania Department of Energy in 2008 indicates a range of increases from as small as 7% to as high as 75% for utilities where rate caps have already expired (see Table 8). By far the largest of these small utilities, Duquesne's rates have increased only 7%.

In the same Fact Sheet, the Pennsylvania Department of Energy also published *anticipated* increases for companies with pending rate cap expirations (see Table 9).

What does this all mean?

In 2008, John Hanger, then president and CEO of PennFuture and Acting Secretary of the Pennsylvania Department of Environmental Protection (he's now the Secretary), speaking to the House

Table 8. Post-rate cap price changes (actual)

	Expired Date	Total Bill Increase
Citizens Electric Of Lewisburg	Dec 31, 2007	35%
Duquesne Light Company	Dec 31, 2003	7%
Pennsylania Power Co. (PennPower) - FirstEnergy Co.	Dec 31, 2006	40%
UGI Utilities Inc.	June 30, 2002	37%
Wellsboro Electric Co.	Jan 2, 2002	31%
Pike County Light & Power Co.	Dec 31, 2005	75%
Source: Pennsylvania DEP Fact Sheet, June 2008.		

	Expiration Date	Anticipated Increases
PPL Electric Utilities	Dec 31, 2009	37%
Allegheny Power (West Penn Power)	Dec 31, 2010	63%
Metropolitan Edison Company (Met-Ed) - FirstEnergy Co.	Dec 31, 2010	54%
PECO Energy Company - Exelon Company	Dec 31, 2010	8%
Pennsylvania Electric Company (Penelec) - FirstEnergy Co.	Dec 31, 2010	50%
Source: Pennsylvania DEP Fact Sheet, June 2008.		

Table 9. Post-rate cap price changes (anticipated)

Consumer Affairs Committee, addressed the issue of electricity pricing after the expiration of rate caps. "Not surprisingly, when electric rates have been capped for as many as 14 years, price increases will occur when the caps expire, even though the increase may not raise rates measured in real or constant dollars when compared to rates charged in 1991 or 1996. Price increases for electricity after rate caps expire are likely to be in the 20% to 50% range."

But even after rate caps expire and that price adjustment is made, other factors will be changing in the future. Hanger points out that after rate caps expire, the price for electricity generation will be set by the markets and there are many factors influencing market prices, including "the amount of supply, the amount of demand, and the costs of inputs like fuel, labor, health care, and materials like steel and concrete for construction of plant."

▓ SMART METERING AND TIME-OF-USE PRICING
By August 2009, utility companies in Pennsylvania must file a plan to procure and implement smart meters. These meters are bi-directional and record your electricity usage at least once an hour.

By January 2010, utilities with 100,000 customers or more must file a plan for offering "time-of-use" or "real time" pricing to customers who have smart meters. These deadlines are for compliance with Act 129.

The basic premise of time-of-use pricing is to charge customers more for the power they use during times of peak demand and less for power they use during times of low demand. The hope is that customers will adjust their usage patterns in a way that is good for regional electricity management. This demand leveling helps the industry operate more reliably, more efficiently and less expensively.

The highest demand for electricity occurs midday during the week in the summer, when air conditioners are running in homes and in businesses. We can all help by changing our behaviors to reduce the electricity we consume during these times. Soon, we'll have the extra motivation of avoiding high prices. We will watch the thermostat more carefully and run the dishwasher at night.

But here's the real kicker: At the very time when demand is peaking and prices are highest, solar electric generators are most productive. This means your solar electric system produces the most electricity at the very time electricity is most needed and of highest value.

Time-of-use pricing will significantly increase the savings and value of the solar electricity we generate during peak demand periods. It is difficult to estimate the extra savings now, until the plans are filed, but time-of-use pricing will clearly work to the advantage of homeowners with solar electric generation systems.

By the way, you can get a smart meter now, if you're willing to pay for it. And smart meters are going into all new construction. Some utilities are already offering pilot time-of-use pricing programs. Check with your local utility for details.

FUTURE ELECTRICITY PRICING, ALL THINGS CONSIDERED

So how much will a solar electric system save me on my power bill? Will it be enough to make this a smart investment for me and my family?

Unfortunately, there is no way to calculate it precisely.

Competition and the introduction of increasingly efficient new generation sources may drive prices down.

On the other hand, increasing demand and the push for cleaner, possibly more expensive, fuel sources may push prices up.

And conservation efforts, smart metering and demand load management may work, driving costs and price down.

Looking at a 25-year window, we may see all these things happen and prices may go up then down and back up, over and over again.

In the middle of all this uncertainty, let's close with some facts:

Once your system is installed, all the electricity it generates for the next 25-plus years will be yours to use *at no charge*. This price you know for sure.

Reducing your power bill—through solar generation and/or energy conservation—is the best way to protect yourself from unexpected swings in power prices.

ESTIMATING FUTURE ELECTRICITY BILL SAVINGS

The amount of money you will save on future electricity bills depends on the amount of electricity your system produces and what you would have paid for that electricity if you had purchased it from the power company. All of the calculations in this chapter can be quickly done for you with the SunnyMoney Estimator, but here's how to do it yourself.

☑ **Annual Electricity Generation**
    To estimate the amount of electricity a system will generate in a year, multiply the system's power rating (kW) by the AC Electricity Generation Factor for its location (kWh/yr for a 1-kW array, see Table 1). The answer will be in kWh.

For example, a 3.2 kW system in Harrisburg,

3.2 kW   x   1,193 kWh/yr/1-kW array   =   3,818 kWh/yr

My estimated annual electricity generation:

_____ kWh/yr

☑ **Future Electricity Bill Savings**
   To estimate future electricity bill savings per year, multiply a
   system's annual electricity generation (kWh/yr) by the
   estimated future price of electricity ($/kWh). The answer will be
   in dollars.

   To estimate future electricity bill savings over the life of the
   system, multiply the annual savings by the number of years.

Continuing the example above and assuming the future price of
electricity is $0.15/kWh,

3,818 kWh/yr x $0.15/kWh = $573/yr

My estimated electricity bill savings per year:

$ _____

Over a 25-year system life, the savings are,

$573/yr x 25 years = $14,325

My estimated electricity bill savings for life of system:

$ _____

Chapter 7
Renewable Energy Credits (RECs)

Also known as:
Alternative Energy Credit (AEC), *official Pennsylvania term*
Solar RECs, S-RECs or SRECs (when specifically for solar)
Green Tags
Tradable Renewable Certificates (TRCs)

Renewable Energy Credits (RECs) give the owners of solar electric systems an opportunity to generate income from their investment. It is a voluntary market mechanism allowing owners to sell the greenness of the electricity they have generated.

A Renewable Energy Credit (REC) is a *certificate* saying that 1 MWh (1,000 kilowatt-hours) of electricity has been generated by an energy source that is renewable and connected to the electrical grid. Residential solar electric systems qualify, with or without battery backup, as long as they are connected to the grid. For each MWh of electricity a solar electric system generates, the owner of that system earns one REC.

Don't read any further until you understand this: The REC is simply a document certifying that green energy was created. It is completely separate from the electricity itself.

Remember buying a pack of baseball cards with a stick of gum? You, or someone, chews the gum, but you still have the cards. You can collect the cards or sell the cards, whatever you like. What you do with the gum and what you do with the cards is completely separate. That's how electricity and RECs work. Electricity is the gum and RECs are the cards.

The purpose of RECs is to give market value to the fact that power was generated from a green source. The physical system that carries electricity from where it is generated to where it is used is called the grid. Power plants of all types generate electricity as needed and send it to the grid. Once it is on the grid, all electricity is the same, whether it came from a wind turbine, a nuclear plant, a hydroelectric plant, a coal-burning plant or a solar panel on grandma's roof. A REC is how we reward the owner of a renewable energy generator for making 1 MWh of green power available to the grid. Every time green power is used to fill grid demand, less electricity needs to be made by conventional sources.

For example, if I want to use green energy at my home and don't have my own green generating capability, here's what I do: I get the energy I need off the grid, just like everyone else. But then I also buy RECs, one for every MWh of electricity I use. This pays someone else to add enough green energy to the grid to cover my usage.

SELLING RECS IS SELLING THE GREEN

Selling your RECs is a choice. You can sell all of your RECs, some of your RECs, or none of your RECs. When you sell a REC, you are selling the green attributes of the electricity it represents. After you sell your RECs, you can no longer legally claim to be using green energy. You are generating green energy that is being used by someone else (whoever paid for the REC).

Having said that, it is also important to note that the income from RECs can make all the difference in a homeowner being able to swing the finances of investing in solar. In many cases, selling RECs is a financial necessity. Many good clean energy projects, both private and commercial, exist only because of the promise of REC income.

VOLUNTARY AND COMPLIANCE REC MARKETS

When an individual or business chooses to go green and buys RECs, they are participating in the **voluntary REC** market. But these are not the only folks buying RECs.

In 2004, Pennsylvania passed Act 213 which requires electric distribution companies and electric generation suppliers to provide a certain percentage of their power from alternative energy sources and specifically from solar sources. The requirements started in 2007 and the percentage gets higher each year until 2021. These companies have to cover their required solar percentage by either generating solar electricity themselves or buying RECs from other solar sources. When power companies buy RECs because they are

53

required to by law, this is referred to as the **compliance REC** market.

Pennsylvania's Alternative Energy Portfolio Standards (AEPS) require that certain amounts of electricity sold to retail customers come from renewable/alternative energy sources. These are divided into Tier I and Tier II (see Table 10).

By May 2021, a minimum of 0.5% of all electricity sold to retail customers in Pennsylvania must come from solar generators. And possibly more, to meet the overall Tier I Requirement (see Table 11).

Table 10. AEPS renewable/alternative energy sources

Tier 1
Energy derived from:
∞ Solar photovoltaic energy
∞ Solar thermal
∞ Wind power
∞ Low-impact hydropower
∞ Geothermal energy
∞ Biologically derived methane gas   (including landfill gas)
∞ Fuel cells
∞ Biomass energy
∞ Coal mine methane
Tier 2
Energy derived from:
∞ Waste coal
∞ Distributed generation systems
∞ Demand-side management
∞ Large-scale hydropower
∞ Municipal solid waste
∞ Generation of electricity utilizing by-products of the pulping process and wood
∞ Integrated combined coal gasification technology

	Percent of Total Electricity Sales		
	Tier I	Solar PV	Tier II
2/28/07 - 5/31/07	1.50%	0.0013%	4.20%
6/1/07 - 5/31/08	1.50%	0.0030%	4.20%
6/1/08 - 5/31/09	2.00%	0.0063%	4.20%
6/1/09 - 5/31/10	2.50%	0.0120%	4.20%
6/1/10 - 5/31/11	3.00%	0.0203%	6.20%
6/1/11 - 5/31/12	3.50%	0.0325%	6.20%
6/1/12 - 5/31/13	4.00%	0.0510%	6.20%
6/1/13 - 5/31/14	4.50%	0.0840%	6.20%
6/1/14 - 5/31/15	5.00%	0.1440%	6.20%
6/1/15 - 5/31/16	5.50%	0.2500%	8.20%
6/1/16 - 5/31/17	6.00%	0.2933%	8.20%
6/1/17 - 5/31/18	6.50%	0.3400%	8.20%
6/1/18 - 5/31/19	7.00%	0.3900%	8.20%
6/1/19 - 5/31/20	7.50%	0.4433%	8.20%
6/1/20 - 5/31/21	8.00%	0.5000%	10.00%

Table 11. AEPS compliance schedule

Some more details about AEPS:

∞ If a company fails to meet its AEPS requirement, it will be assessed an alternative compliance payment (ACP). In the special case of solar compliance, the ACP is "200% of average market value" of solar credits (S-RECs) sold during the reporting period.

∞ In Chapter 6 we talked about rate caps on electricity prices and presented a schedule showing when the rate caps would expire for each utility (see Table 6) . This same schedule applies to compliance with AEPS. When rate caps expire is also when utility companies must start to meet Pennsylvania's standards for alternative energies. For the largest utilities this will happen at the end of 2009 and 2010.

∞ In the compliance market, a REC is "good" the year it is created and for two additional compliance years.

∞ For solar electric systems under 15 kW, the number of RECs created can be based on estimates of the amount of electricity generated, without a special meter measuring exactly how much your system produced.

COUNTING YOUR RECS

The number of RECs your system will create is based on the amount of electricity your system generates.

☑ **Number of RECs per Year**

To estimate the number of RECs your system will create per year, divide the system's annual electricity generation in (kWh/yr) by 1,000. Answer will be in RECs/yr.

My estimated number of RECs per year:

_____ RECs/yr

To roughly estimate your generation, multiply your system's power rating times the AC Electricity Generation factor for your location, see Table 1.

For example, if you have a 6 kW system installed in Pittsburgh,

6 kW x $\dfrac{\text{1,099 kWh/year}}{\text{1 installed kW}}$ = 6,594 kWh/yr

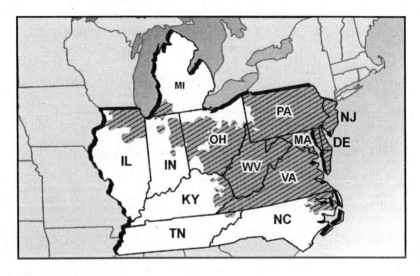

Figure 10. PJM region map

One REC is 1,000 kWh. The number of RECs generated by this system is,

6,594 kWh/yr x $\frac{1 \text{ REC}}{1,000 \text{ kWh}}$ = 6.6 RECs/yr

⌨ HOW RECS ARE BOUGHT AND SOLD

Renewable Energy Credits are traded on the open market. An owner, or someone representing the owner, lets the world know that RECs are available and then those interested in buying the RECs make an offer. For compliance trades especially, this happens in a highly controlled marketplace.

To qualify your RECs to be sold in the compliance market, your solar electric system must be registered with Pennsylvania's AEPS program.

This program is administered by Clean Power Markets. They manage the web portal where your facility is registered and managed. It is here that your RECs are created, based on the production estimates for your system.

To sell your RECs on the compliance market, they must be deposited into a PJM-GATS account. PJM is the regional transmission operator for our part of the national power grid. The PJM region includes Pennsylvania and all or part of nine other states and the District of Columbia (see Figure 10).

GATS stands for Generation Attribute Tracking System and is the on-line electronic marketplace where solar RECs (and others) are controlled and their trades monitored. The financial transaction happens outside of GATS, but GATS is where ownership, generation source, age, and other REC attributes are officially maintained.

When a link has been established between your Clean Power Markets account and a PJM-GATS account, your RECs will be automatically deposited into the GATS account where they can be made available for sale.

You can do all of this on your own. You can register your solar electric generator with AEPS and set up your own GATS account from which you can sell your RECs. These systems are complicated, but training is available. And it will require attention on your part to monitor your accounts, find buyers and execute trades.

Earlier in this chapter, we gave an example of a 6 kW residential solar electric system that created about 6.6 RECs per year. For the individual home owner, this is a substantial number but to a utility looking to buy hundreds or thousands of RECs, six is pocket change. These big players will prefer to buy RECs in large blocks, requiring fewer negotiations and fewer transactions.

REC AGGREGATORS

Aggregators are service providers who work with many small individual generators to bundle their RECs together and market them as one large block or lot to large buyers. For the residential solar electric owner, this provides a low-hassle path to market and increases the likelihood that a buyer will be found for their RECs and probably increases the negotiating power and price the owner will receive for the RECs.

Generally speaking, there are two ways to do business with an aggregator. In a **fixed-price** arrangement you commit to sell and the aggregator commits to buy your RECs at a pre-determined price, regardless of the current market price. This gives you the assurance of steady income, but probably causes you to miss some value if REC prices increase. Of course, the aggregator is betting on REC prices increasing, so that your RECs can be resold at a profit.

In the other **fee-based** or **commission** arrangement you and the aggregator agree that they will sell your RECs at the best market price. In return, the aggregator keeps a percentage of the revenue or a flat fee, depending on your agreement. You and the aggregator share the risks and rewards of open market pricing. If prices soar, you're in good shape. If not, well...

With SunnyMoney, you can estimate your REC income using fixed-price or market value with a commission.

There are no requirements for an aggregator to be registered or licensed. It's up to you to check references and read contracts carefully. The state's Alternative Energy Portfolio Standards website maintains a list of self-reported aggregators doing business in Pennsylvania.

REC PRICES
RECs in New Jersey, which has an established REC market, have been selling for more than $600 each. In Pennsylvania, current reported prices for solar RECS are around $230 and aggregators are offering fixed-price contacts in this ballpark.

Future prices? The dog swallowed my crystal ball. Seriously, projections are all over the place but no one can predict future markets with any certainty. If you enter into a fixed-price agreement with an aggregator, you will know the future value of your RECs. Otherwise, it's your best guesstimate.

S-REC MARKET LIFE
At the time of this writing, the Pennsylvania solar REC market is in its infancy. Some points to consider:

∞ For the largest utility companies, the compliance to Alternative Energy Portfolio Standards doesn't begin until the end of 2009 and 2010.

∞ Current Alternative Energy Portfolio Standards expire in 2021, but that may be changing on the state and national level.

∞ Solar RECs have a shelf life of less than three years—the compliance year they are created, plus two more.

∞ A solar electric system installed in 2009 can be expected to last through 2034, or longer.

ESTIMATING YOUR INCOME FROM RECS
The amount of money you make from selling RECs will depend somewhat on how you sell them.

∞ If you are selling them yourself, the net income per REC is simply the market value, assuming your outside costs to make the trade are minimal.

∞ If you have a fixed-price contract, the net income per REC will be the price you have agreed upon with your aggregator.

∞ If you have a fee or commission based contract with an aggregator, net income per REC will be market value less the commission or fee.

When estimating income from RECs, you also need to consider the number of years you expect to sell RECs at this price. Do you think the market will materialize soon? Will it end in 2021, or continue? Do you think you'll be able to sell RECs over the full life of the system?

Remember you can do these calculations automatically with the SunnyMoney Estimator.

☑ REC Income

To estimate REC income per year, multiply the number of RECs per year by the net income per REC. The answer will be in $/yr.

To estimate REC income over the life of the system, multiply REC income per year by the number of years you expect to sell RECs. The answer will be in $.

My estimated REC income per year:

_____ $/yr

My estimated REC income over the life of the system:

$ _____

Important Note about RECs and Taxes

REC income is likely taxable at both the federal and state level. Please consult a professional tax advisor.

Chapter 8
For Love *and* Money?

Even with generous incentives, a solar electric system is a significant investment for most of us. It's not something we have to do, but something we chose to do, each for our own reasons.

When we buy a car, there are many factors to consider—fuel efficiency, fuel type, safety, cost, reliability, capacity, appearance, source country, manual/automatic transmission, convertible, four-wheel drive, sound system, DVD players, even cup holders... We each have our own formula for what factors matter most. For some, safety at all cost. For others, it must be a hybrid. When I was a kid, it was easy—it had to be a Chevy!

But for most of us, it's a combination of factors. We care about cost AND safety AND efficiency AND comfort and we develop our own mental scale about how to balance all of these and reach a decision. And then for some, it's just love at first sight. My sisters (both of them!) and PT Cruisers. As long as they could make the payments, it was the car for them.

Similarly, the decision to purchase a solar electric system presents many possible factors to consider. Some can be easily measured, some cannot. They all matter; they just matter to each of us differently. This chapter will help you understand the facts behind the factors. Only you know how much each one means to you.

ENVIRONMENT
According to the Environmental Protection Agency, every 1,000 kWh of electricity saved results in 0.79 tons of avoided carbon dioxide emissions. For a 4 kW solar electric system in Pennsylvania, which could be expected to generate about 4,800 kWh of electricity per year, the total emissions avoided would be about 3.8 tons of carbon dioxide per year, or **95 tons** over the 25-yr life of the system.

But, we don't usually go around thinking or talking about tons of carbon dioxide. So here are some equivalents, again from the EPA.

For each year, the electricity saved by a 4 kW solar electric system equals:

∞ Annual greenhouse gas emissions from 0.63 passenger vehicles or

∞ CO_2 emissions from 391 gallons of gasoline, or

∞ CO_2 emissions from 8 barrels of oil, or

∞ CO_2 emissions from the electricity use of 0.48 homes for one year, or

∞ Carbon sequestered by 88.4 tree seedlings grown for 10 years, or

∞ Carbon sequestered annually by 0.78 acres of pine or fir forests, or

∞ Greenhouse gas emissions avoided by recycling 1.2 tons of waste instead of sending it to the landfill

These benefits will continue for 25 years or more.

HOME IMPROVEMENT

In a recent publication, the Department of Energy cites a report that a solar electric system increases your home's value by $20 for every $1 in annual utility bill savings. Assuming the average price of electricity in Pennsylvania is $0.11 kWh, the 4-kW system described above would save $528 per year, increasing the appraisal value of your home by $10,560. The full installation cost for this system would have been about $12,000, assuming a price of $7.50/W, and qualification for the Pennsylvania Sunshine Solar Rebate and the Federal Tax Credit.

PATRIOTIC

The events of September 11, 2001 opened our eyes to "petroeconomics" and the policies, principals and practices often fueled with the money we spend on foreign oil. More recently, soaring oil prices reminded us of our country's vulnerability to powers beyond our borders. This country is built on a spirit of independence, resourcefulness and self-responsibility. For many of us, taking steps to reduce our personal use of foreign oil is a matter of patriotic duty to keep ourselves and our country strong, healthy and out of harm's way.

In our part of the country, most electricity is generated from coal-burning or nuclear plants. It is energy from these sources, not oil, that will most likely be displaced by electricity we generate on our own roofs and yards. But the availability of clean local electricity may influence our future choices, such as the cars we drive and how we heat our homes. Solar energy helps displace our long-term dependence on petroleum from other countries and environmentally fragile sources.

SELF RELIANCE
How gratifying is it to eat the vegetables you grew, hang the curtains you made, drive the car you repaired, see the house you painted, burn the wood you split, eat the pie you made from scratch? If these things rock your boat, you probably love the idea of turning sunshine into electricity, saving money and reducing your dependence on the power company. And it's especially appealing in Pennsylvania where little maintenance is required; so once it's done it's done and you can enjoy the fruits and freedom of solar-generated electricity for 25 years or more with little trouble or expense.

CERTAINTY
The one sure way to protect yourself against future increases in the price of electricity is to reduce the amount of electricity you buy from the power company. Solar generation coupled with energy conservation will help you bring certainty to your future power bills.

When you install a solar electric system, you now *know* how much you will pay for solar electricity for the next 25 years or more. With near certainty, you know the one-time cost for your system and how much electricity it will generate. In effect, it gives you the ability to lock in pricing for all or part of your future electricity needs.

Now, with the state and federal incentives (even without potential REC income), the price of electricity from solar sources and public utilities is nearly the same. This "grid parity," a long-time goal of solar advocates, is now a reality.

FINANCIAL ANALYSIS

Whether you're talking solar energy or a new car, cost is one factor that matters to nearly all of us. Only you know how important the cost is to you and your family, especially relative to the other factors. This section shows some ways to consider the financial aspects of a solar electric system that may be helpful.

Please remember that all the calculations presented in this section can be done for you automatically by the SunnyMoney Estimator. The methods and examples are presented here to help you interpret the results and do the math yourself, if you wish.

Payback Period

The payback period is the amount of time it will take for you to "pay off" your system with savings on your power bills and REC income (if you sell your RECs).

Payback Period (yrs) =

$$\frac{\$ \text{ Net Cost}}{\$ \text{ Annual Electricity Bill Savings} + \$ \text{ Annual REC Income}}$$

For example (using assumed data),

$$\frac{\$12,700}{(\$592 + \$733)/\text{yr}} = \textbf{9.6 years}$$

This is a simple and common calculation, but really not very useful as a decision-making tool. It tells you when you'll "get your money back" but it does not take into account what happens after that.

In this case, the calculation tells us the system will have "paid for itself" in less than 10 years, but what about the next 15 or 20 years of savings that will come from this system? Those benefits, in fact most of the benefits of this investment, do not show up in a payback calculation. And, the payback period calculation does not take into account the time value of money.

Finally, the payback period doesn't really help us decide—compared to what? We don't say, "At our house we only invest in projects with a payback period of less than 6 years."

So payback period is an easy and understandable number, but not your best bet for deciding.

Simple Return on Investment (ROI)

Another common financial measure is Return on Investment, which is simply the ratio of how much your investment returns each year divided by how much it cost initially.

ROI % =

$$\frac{\$ \text{ Annual Electricity Bill Savings} + \$ \text{ Annual REC Income}}{\$ \text{ Net Cost}}$$

For example (using the same assumed data),

$$\frac{\$592 + \$733}{\$12,700} = \mathbf{10.4\%}$$

You'll notice that ROI is the reciprocal of payback period. (The same fraction, flipped over.) ROI has many of the same drawbacks as payback—it doesn't reflect that the benefits continue for 25 or more years, and doesn't take into account the changing value of money over time. On the other hand, as a percentage representing a "return," ROI represents a familiar concept that we can relate to other types of investments.

The Time Value of Money

The "time value of money" refers to the fact that a dollar today is worth more than a dollar tomorrow. If you have $100 today and put it into a bank account that pays an interest rate of 1.5%, then a year from now you will have $101.50. Similarly, if you borrow money today it will cost you more when you pay it pack later.

Here's the basic equation,

$$FV_n = PV(1 + r)^n$$
FV = Future Value ($)
PV = Present Value ($)
R = rate of interest
N = period (the year, with the beginning of the project being year zero)

In the example above, $101.50 $=$ $100 x (1 + 0.015)^1

When you purchase a solar electric system for your home, you pay out one big chunk of money. In about 60 days, you get a chunk back from the state and the next time you pay federal taxes you get another chunk back in the form of tax credits. After that, it's a steady trickle of savings on your electrical bill, month after month, for 25 years or more, and, if you choose, a stream of REC income year after year.

From a financial analysis point of view, the challenge is how to compare the dollars you spend now with the value of all those dollars in savings and income you expect over the next 25-plus years.

To consider the time value of money, you need to model the cash going out and the cash coming in each year over the life of your system. For a solar electric installation, you know how much your system costs, and can estimate the cost to replace the inverter in 15 years. The harder part is estimating your future electricity bill savings and your future income from RECs, if you choose to sell them.

Once this cash flow is modeled, you can use different analyses to evaluate the investment value of the project. We'll consider Internal Rate of Return and Net Present Value.

Internal Rate of Return (IRR)

One measure for looking at dollars today and tomorrow is the Internal Rate of Return. This calculation gives you a rate (you can think of it as interest) of how hard your money is working for you.

Imagine that, instead of buying a solar electric system, you loaned the money to someone and they paid you back over a long time with interest. You don't know what the interest rate is, but you do know what size payments they will make and for how long. You can use this information to calculate the interest rate. That is what the Internal Rate of Return calculation does.

If you'd like to do it yourself, Microsoft Excel has a built in IRR function with good "Help" information. Or, visit the on-line SunnyMoney Estimator.

Interpreting IRR. IRR is a useful number because it can help you compare to other investment options. Your solar electric purchase is considered a long-term, low risk investment that will generate electricity reliably for 25 years or longer. From an analysis point of view, the risk comes in your assumptions about future electricity prices and REC income.

The higher the IRR the better the return on your investment. How high is necessary for you and your household? There is no one magic number. What could you do with this same money elsewhere, over the same time period with the same level of risk? What other low-risk investments would benefit you, the environment, national security and economy and increase your home value?

Net Present Value (NPV)

Like IRR, the Net Present Value takes into account the time value of money. The NPV calculation looks at all the cash flows over time, but in this case you provide the interest rate that describes the value of future dollars relative to today's dollars. For the purposes of NPV calculations, this rate is called the "discount rate."

In the example above, we put $100 in the bank now and got $101.50 back a year later, because a dollar today is worth more than a dollar a year from now.

The result of an NPV calculation is a dollar value which tells you the current value of the cash flow, taking into account the time value of money based on the discount rate. The IRR is the discount rate that causes NPV to be zero.

Consider this example: Putting in $100 and getting back $101.50 a year later means the IRR is 1.5%. Your investment is earning 1.5%. The discount rate is 1.5%. The calculation would tell us that the NPV is $0. When you consider the time value of money and a discount rate of 1.5%, all the cash flow out and all the cash flow in add up to zero. Your investment is earning exactly 1.5%, nothing more or less.

Okay, but what if you got back *more than* $101.50? This is a positive NPV. The investment is earning 1.5%, and then some. That extra amount, in current dollars, is the NPV. Similarly, if you got back less than $101.50 then you're not even making the 1.5%, the discount value; the NPV is negative.

What should you use for discount value? The idea is to reflect the future value of money *to you*. If you are carrying debt, such as a mortgage, use the highest interest rate you are paying. If no debt, then consider the interest you could get from other low-risk long-term investments, such as a government bond. You can easily look up the interest rate for 10-year treasury bonds, which is currently around 3.5%.

If you'd like to do it yourself, Microsoft Excel has a built-in NPV function with good "Help" information. Or, visit the on-line SunnyMoney Estimator.

Interpreting NPV. A positive NPV means that your project is outperforming the discount rate you specified. The higher the NPV the better. We don't often use measures like NPV in our personal budgeting process, and it may be a little tough to relate this number to your decision making. For an NPV of $5,000 on a $38,000 project with a 4% discount rate, you could think of it this way: "If someone promised me a $5,000 bonus to put $38,000 in an account earning 4% for the next 25 years, would I do it?"

"Price to Beat," the known price of your solar electricity
This is the price you will pay for the solar electricity you generate
from your roof or yard. It is a fixed, known price that won't change
for the life of the system (25 years or more).

Price ($/kWh) =

$ Net Cost + $ Replace inverter – $ REC income over system life
Annual Solar Generation x 25 years

For example (using assumed data), the price to beat is,

$12,700 + $2,800 - ($733 x 12) = **$0.06 / kWh**
4,736 kWh/yr x 25 years

A more sophisticated solution involves using a discount rate to
adjust for the fact that future dollars are worth less than current
dollars. The equation above stays the same, but you use the Net
Present Value of all the cash flows (Net Cost, Inverter Cost and
REC income).

This calculation is also available in the on-line SunnyMoney
Estimator.

Both methods (simple and discounted cash flow) provide useful
information to help you evaluate the investment potential of a solar
electric purchase.

Interpreting Price to Beat. Price-to-Beat is a very useful number
because you can compare it to the price you pay for electricity now
and expect to pay in the future. If, for example, you had the chance
to lock in electricity prices at $0.06/kWh for the next 25 years,
would you take it? What if you are currently paying the power
company $0.10/kWh? What if you expect prices to go up 20%, to
$0.12/kWh? This is an understandable and real basis for
comparison.

Bottom line: Once you pay to have your system installed, the
electricity it generates is yours free to use for the life of the system,
25 years or longer.

Chapter 9
Installation Process

Having a solar electric system professionally installed on your property is an interesting and rewarding project.

BEFORE CONTACTING AN INSTALLER
It will be very helpful to you both if you have the following:

∞   A power bill showing your annual electricity usage (kWh)

∞   Ideas for one or more possible locations on your property that are *unshaded* and south facing

∞   Your budget

∞   An understanding of how the state rebates and federal tax incentives work

∞   An understanding of what RECs are and how you can make money from them

∞   Results from some costs/benefits analyses (like SunnyMoney) to help you understand the possible size, costs and benefits of a system that may work for your property and budget.

CONTACT INSTALLERS AND OBTAIN PROPOSALS
To qualify for a Pennsylvania Sunshine rebate, you *must* use an installer from the state's list of approved installers.

The installer will probably do a "pre-qualification" interview with you on the phone to understand your project and check its overall viability. As part of this interview, the installer may use a website (such as Google Earth) to look at images of your property and be sure there is a location for your array that is large enough, unshaded and south facing.

Before preparing a proposal, the installer will visit your property. During this site visit, the installer will do a shading analysis, take measurements, and check out your electrical service. Installers may charge a small fee to perform a site assessment, which may later be credited if you choose to do the project with them. The site assessment is an important part of your project. It takes your installer time and costs money to do it well.

Proposals

It is recommended that you get at least two or three proposals. Each proposal should include, at a minimum:

∞ Estimated system performance—system power rating (kW) and the amount of electricity you can expect to generate

∞ Planned location of array(s), inverter, production meter and any other included components

∞ Mounting and racking description

∞ Trenching plans and landscape repair

∞ Component descriptions—manufacturer and model numbers for modules and inverter

∞ Commitment to qualify for and fulfill Pennsylvania Sunshine Rebate requirements

∞ Costs for all material and labor

∞ Fees associated with permits, applications

∞ Payment schedule

∞ Proof of Workers Compensation Insurance and Commercial General Liability Insurance.

∞ Copy of Pennsylvania Contractor License

∞ Contractor's 5-year warranty for parts and labor, including who is responsible for the cost of removing, shipping, reinstalling or replacing any defective components. (This is required for the Pennsylvania Sunshine Rebate)

SELECT INSTALLER AND PROPOSAL

To select an installer, consider the following:

∞ Price. The average cost for installed solar electric in Pennsylvania is in the range of $7 to $10/W. If proposed price is outside of this range, ask for an explanation.

∞ Payment schedule. It is reasonable for an installer to expect a substantial portion upfront to help cover the costs of materials that need to be ordered on your behalf. But, it is also reasonable for a substantial final payment to be due and paid only after the installation has passed all necessary inspections and all paperwork is complete.

∞ System design and component selection, including where manufactured, if you prefer USA made.

∞ Installation schedule. Remember, to qualify for the state rebate, the installation must be complete within 12 months of receiving rebate pre-approval. One 30-day extension may be requested.

∞ Completeness of proposal.

∞ Contractor's warranty.

∞ Promptness, reliability. Were phone calls returned, emails answered, appointments on time and commitments kept?

∞ References. Ask for three references of previous customers that you can call or visit, then do it.

∞ Knowledge and experience. Your installer should understand the technology and have the ability to explain it clearly and should be comfortable with filing applications, acquiring permits, and interacting with utilities.

∞ Cash flow. You and the installer should be very clear about your cash flow—the amount of each payment and when it is due, when your rebate will be received, and any financing arrangements.

The Pennsylvania Sunshine Rebate program requires that a solar photovoltaic installation company have at least one "qualified employee" on staff. This screening helps ensure that the installers you contact are capable and prepared to do your project. But don't rely on this entirely; things change. Be sure to check references, contact the Better Business Bureau and use your good judgment.

🖳 BEFORE INSTALLATION
Pennsylvania Solar Rebate: Pre-Approval

The application process to apply for the Pennsylvania Solar Rebate involves two steps, both of which must be done by the installer. The application is done through an on-line process available only to installers who are on the state Department of Environmental Protection list.

The first step is to submit a Pre-Approval Application that will determine whether your project is eligible for the rebate and how much it will be. If your project is approved, the rebate money is reserved for you and you have 12 months to finish the project. You may apply for one 30-day extension.

Before applying for a rebate, the program requires you pay an installer deposit of $250 at minimum. Your installer will complete an on-line application with details about the system owner (you), project site and components. Your installer will also provide the following:

∞ Manufacturer's specification for all components.

∞ Project cost estimate, purchase order or letter of intent.

∞ Shading analysis (produced by Solar Pathfinder, Solmetric or Wiley Asset) showing that a minimum of 80% optimal production is expected from the system.

∞ System schematic or line drawing.

∞ Plot plan showing the location of the PV array, inverter and point of interconnection on the property.

∞ For rooftop installations, a diagram illustrating the roof dimensions, location of PV modules, orientation and tilt of PV modules.

Administrators of Pennsylvania's Sunshine Solar Program expect the process time for pre-approval applications to be about four weeks. They will notify you directly when your project is pre-approved for the state rebate. They will also notify your installer.

Grid Interconnect Application

Your installer will file an interconnection application and related design documents with your local utility requesting approval to interconnect your planned solar electric generation system to the grid. You'll need to sign the application.

Local Permits and Zoning Approvals

In Pennsylvania, each municipality is responsible for its own permitting rules. Your installer will need to check with local authorities to understand permitting requirements and zoning ordinances that may apply to your property and solar electric project. However, it is your property and your neighborhood, so you too need to understand the requirements and any issues. The installer will need to comply on your behalf with all aspects of these regulations.

DURING INSTALLATION

Be nice, take pictures, have fun!

AFTER INSTALLATION

Local Inspections and Zoning Approvals

If your local authorities require electrical or building permits, inspections need to be performed and approvals received upon completion of the project. Also, any zoning approvals should be documented.

Grid Interconnect Completion

Your installer will file a certificate of completion application/agreement, with proof of electrical inspection, and a net energy metering rider application. You'll need to sign the applications. Upon approval, the utility will replace your meter with a bi-directional meter, or add a second meter to accomplish the same function, at no additional cost to you.

Pennsylvania Solar Rebate: Request Reimbursement

After the project is completed, your installer will submit a Post-Installation Reimbursement Application to request that the rebate be paid. Once again, this can only be done by your installer. The reimbursement request is done through the on-line process available only to qualified installers who are on the state DEP list.

The installer will have to provide proof that your solar electric system meets these requirements:

∞ System was installed according to industry and code standards and as specified in the equipment manufacturer's manual.

∞ Any applicable local government permits and zoning approvals have been obtained.

∞ The installed system complies with the Pennsylvania Uniform Construction Code and all local laws and codes.

The installer will also have to provide the following:

∞ Copies of the manufacturers' and contractor's labor warranties. Equipment must carry a 5 year warranty for inverters and 20-year warranty for solar panels. In addition, to manufacturer's warranties on specific components, the contractor must provide a full 5-year warranty for all parts and labor, plus the cost of removing, shipping and reinstalling or replacing a defective component. A warranty statement, included in the contract, will clearly state who is responsible for labor, material and shipment of defective parts.

∞ PV interconnection and net metering paperwork must be completed and approved by utility. If your home is independent of the grid, you may request an exception from this which the department will evaluate on a case-by-case basis.

∞ Project Completion Form signed by applicant and contractor.

∞ Copies of electrical or building permit inspection approvals, where applicable.

∞ Copy of final sales invoice.

When filing your Request for Reimbursement, the installer is allowed to mark your invoice as "unpaid." This gives you and the installer *the option* to work out an agreement where the balance of the cost is due when the rebate reimbursement is received. In all cases the rebate check will go directly to the homeowner. Program

Administrators expect reimbursement payments to be issued within 60 days of receiving a fully completed reimbursement request.

Owner's Manual

As required by the Pennsylvania Sunshine Rebate program, the installer must provide you with the following documentation:

∞ Name and address of the seller (installer)

∞ System model name or number

∞ Identification and explanation of system components

∞ Single line drawing of the system

∞ Description of system operation

∞ Description of system maintenance

∞ Description of emergency procedures

∞ Procedures for vacation or extended time away from the building

∞ Contractor's parts and labor warranty

∞ Copies of manufacturers' warranties for major system components

∞ Manufactures' users manuals

Federal Income Tax Credit

At the time of this writing, the 2009 tax forms and instructions for the Federal Residential Renewable Energy Tax Credit have not yet been released. To receive this tax credit, you should consult with a tax professional and include Form 5695 with your next federal tax filings. You will need to provide the amount of your "Qualified Solar Electric Property Costs." The 2008 instructions described these costs as follows:

> ...costs for property that uses solar energy to generate electricity for use in your home located in the United States. This includes costs relating to a solar panel or other property installed as a roof or a portion of a roof. The home does not have to be your main home.

RECs

In Pennsylvania, RECs are called Alternative Energy Credits (AECs). Regardless of when your system was installed and put into operation, your AECs don't begin to accumulate until you have completed an application to qualify it with the state as an alternative energy system.

If you choose to sell all or some of your AECs, or if you would just like to have the option, you'll need to be registered as an alternative energy system in Pennsylvania's program for Alternative Energy Portfolio Standards. The process is administered by Clean Power Markets, Inc. To sell your RECs on the compliance market, they will also need to be available on the PJM-GATS system.

While you can sell your RECs yourself, working with an aggregator greatly simplifies the process of selling your RECs. A good aggregator will handle your accounts for you and conduct transactions on your behalf.

Registering your system and getting AECs on the market is your responsibility, though some installers may offer advice or services. Don't forget this important step if REC income is important to you!

EPILOGUE

This book has covered a lot of ground, especially for folks new to solar electricity. It is a learning curve, but an interesting and enlightening one. Okay, let's just say it—empowering!

You'll have questions along the way. Visit this book's companion website for more information and essential up-to-date details for residential solar installations in Pennsylvania.

To access the website, visit **www.themarea.org.**

You'll find links to data that is likely to change and other on-line resources, including certified installers, rebate levels, calculators, program requirements, downloadable forms and documents, reference material and more. And of course, access to **SunnyMoney**, the solar electric estimating calculator for Pennsylvania homeowners. If you choose, the website will also notify you of announcements or changes that may affect your project.

With the purchase of this book, you have supported the Mid-Atlantic Renewable Energy Association. MAREA is a nonprofit organization, dedicated to informing and educating the public on renewable energy production, energy efficiency, and sustainable living through meetings, workshops, educational materials and energy fairs. Thank you.

For more information and to join, please visit **www.themarea.org.**

To understand solar energy and its value, we pause to be fully aware of the sun and how it moves through our daily world. We really see the shade in our yard, the pitch of our roof. We think about the electricity in our house, always available any time at any outlet. Where does it come from? At what cost to me, to us, to the environment? And when we're done, we can't help but find ourselves considering our choices and gently thinking about who we are and life's priorities.

On a personal note, I hope the journey guided here brings you many unexpected gifts that are simple and pleasing.

M·A·R·E·A
MIDATLANTIC RENEWABLE ENERGY ASSOC.

Celebrating Local and Green

Congratulations! With your purchase of this book, you've supported Pennsylvania businesses and organizations committed to the environment and sustainable living. The Mid-Atlantic Renewable Energy Association is delighted to share green bragging rights. Oh the possibilities!

■ This book has been 100% designed, produced and printed in *Pennsylvania* for Pennsylvania.

■ The book and cover are printed on recycled paper that contains *100% post-consumer waste* and is *Processed Chlorine Free*.

■ This paper is certified by the *Forestry Stewardship Council.*

■ The cover paper is also *Green Seal* certified and was manufactured with *wind-generated energy.*

■ The manufacturer of the paper used for the book pages is powered by *biogas*. And this paper carries the *EcoLogo*.

The paper used for the book and its cover meets the highest international standards for environmental and social responsibility.

100% PCW